ANNAPOLIS
AUTUMN

ANNAPOLIS AUTUMN

Life, Death, and Literature
at the U.S. Naval Academy

BRUCE FLEMING

THE NEW PRESS

NEW YORK
LONDON

Requests for permission to reproduce selections from this book should be mailed to:
Permissions Department, The New Press, 38 Greene Street, New York, NY 10013.

Published in the United States by The New Press, New York, 2005
Distributed by W. W. Norton & Company, Inc., New York

Portions of this book originally appeared, in slightly different form, in the *Chronicle of Higher Education*, the *Antioch Review*, and the *Southwest Review*.

LIBRARY OF CONGRESS CATALOGING-IN-PUBLICATION DATA

Fleming, Bruce E. (Bruce Edward), 1954–
    Annapolis autumn : life, death, and literature at the U.S. Naval Academy /
Bruce Fleming.
        p.   cm.
    ISBN 1-59558-002-6 (hc.)
    1. United States Naval Academy.   2. Fleming, Bruce E. (Bruce Edward),
1954–   3. College teachers—Maryland—Annapolis—Biography.   4. English
literature—Study and teaching—Maryland—Annapolis.   5. Annapolis (Md.)
—Biography.   I. Title.

V415.P1F54   2005
359'.0092—dc22   2005041480

The New Press was established in 1990 as a not-for-profit alternative to the large,
commercial publishing houses currently dominating the book publishing industry.
The New Press operates in the public interest rather than for private gain, and is
committed to publishing, in innovative ways, works of educational, cultural, and
community value that are often deemed insufficiently profitable.

www.thenewpress.com

Composition by dix!

Printed in the United States of America

10   9   8   7   6   5   4   3   2   1

To the Brigade of Midshipmen

and to the memory

of my brother Keith

Lass uns menschlich sein.—

(Let's just all try to be human.—)

—Ludwig Wittgenstein,
Vermischte Bemerkungen (1937)

ANNAPOLIS
AUTUMN

I

Apotheosis

COMMISSIONING WEEK AT the U.S. Naval Academy, where for almost two decades I have taught English to midshipmen—students in training to become officers in the U.S. Navy or Marine Corps—is a riot of pageantry. Its sounds range from the grunts of sweating, half-naked students covered with lard and dirt trying to put a cap on the Herndon obelisk to the ceremonial pomp of blank gunshots fired as salutes to visiting admirals at the Color Parade, salutes that leave trailing after-plumes and a haze of acridity floating out across the water. Its colors divide out into a spectrum of the red, blue, and yellow-striped bellies of the spinnakers on the sailboats sailing up and back just for show on the sky-blue Severn, and reunite in the blinding whites of the summer uniforms reflecting the sun and causing viewers to shade their eyes. Its feels include the heat-trapping, constricting parade jackets for which midshipmen are fitted as first-year plebes that now are too small, to the thud of the ceremonial swords clanking against their thighs, to the exhilarated pump of their arms as they toss their hats high into the sky.

Once this festive week was called June Week, but for a number of years the ceremonies have taken place in May, and "May Week" clearly lacks the same ring. The Commissioning Week rituals themselves begin with the Plebe Recognition Ceremony at Herndon Monument, where the entire plebe class spends hours trying to scale the greased obelisk, and culminate in the Color Parade and Graduation Day. Awards ceremonies, church services, and morning formations punctuate the rest of the week, held together by the celebration of the officers-to-be.

One mid-May day, as if there were any danger of my forgetting that Commissioning Week is almost upon us—it's all the students have been talking about for months—I find in my mailbox a program for the ceremonies. I know what this brochure is without opening it, for on its cover is a photograph of the hat toss that ends the graduation ceremonies so spectacularly: a chair-level shot of jubilant young men and a few women leaping into the air in their "choker white" uniforms—so called because of their Nehru collars (as they were baptized in the West in the 1960s) and, of course, their color—the sky full of the snow-white discs of their "covers." The hat toss is the apogee of Graduation Day, and pictures of it are more to the point than the event itself, as they are always taken at its most orgasmic moment, and do not show what happens either before or after. Before, perhaps unsurprisingly, is more fun. The program, that I add to a pile of papers, flyers, and letters to be answered on the corner of my desk, is printed with thousands of Benday dots, all in blue on the tan paper. I hold it up to the light to admire the effect of tessellation as I move it up to my eyes, my own private Impressionist painting.

First, each Graduation Day, weather permitting, the Blue Angels, the Navy's stunt-pilot team, are announced, and we wait breathlessly. People hear them coming and turn excitedly to their neighbors. The nearly inaudible sound grows louder. Suddenly they appear, trailing huge fluffy white tails. They streak over Navy–Marine Corps Memorial Stadium, where all this takes place. The crowd cheers. Then the planes are over the back of the stadium and disappear into the blue.

A few days before, they have given a full program to the Annapolitans craning their necks from lawn chairs on the Academy grounds and sloping lawns all up and down the Severn, slowing traffic on the main Route 50 highway to Washington as rubberneckers gaze upward. The six planes fly at each other, playing chicken, and turn sideways at the last moment. Three fly against two, and then the reverse. They fly upside down. They loop the loop. Their best trick is what I think of as the bouquet, where the planes fly straight up into the sky and curve outward as they ascend, like a bunch of flowers from a vase, with their jet trails marking their paths.

After the planes leave on Graduation Day, we get down to business. Opening remarks are made. God the Father is invoked. The President, or the Secretary of Defense, or the Secretary of the Navy delivers a speech. Then comes the longest single component in this day's activities, the passage across the stage of the graduates, all sitting now in a gleaming white-clad block in the center of the football field.

When I first came to the Academy, this part took an hour and a half. With the downsizing of the Brigade, the student body, in the 1990s from a high of about 4,500 to closer to 4,000, we had gotten it down to about an hour. The Brigade has begun to swell again, and we're drifting back up to an hour and a quarter. Until recently, we faculty members sat sweating under our mortarboards, shifting uncomfortably on our metal chairs, talking, keeping ourselves amused as best we could for this period of time by looking idly for favorite students. Now, there are "hospitality tents" down on the field. After the first hundred honors graduates get their diplomas, in order of merit, we are free to leap from our seats—no eyes are on us anyway—and spend the rest of the time allotted to awarding of diplomas to the once 36, now 30 companies, into which the Brigade is divided, sipping over-sweet iced tea or bottled water in the shade.

The parents at least have the goal of waiting for their own child to graduate. Pity those with children in the first company! When the students receive their diplomas, they whoop and shout, some jumping into the air to do a kick, or throwing triumphant fists at the sky. This too is a photographic moment much loved by the newspapers, with the Commander-in-Chief or other brass in the background. In the stands, their friends and families cheer, each midshipman's entourage for him or her when their graduate's name is called. Some of the family members blow football-game foghorns and brandish oversized foam hands. All this is a tradition; the Superintendent reminds them in his remarks that they are not only free, but encouraged, to be so indecorous. For an hour and a quarter, the sound of cheering drifts from spot to spot, from side to side across the stadium, like a fire flaring up and being put out, a continuous stream of noise that alters in intensity depending on the size and location of the individual student's claque.

At some point that seems random, the entire class erupts in wild applause at one student's name: this is the "anchorman," the student who, while nonetheless graduating, has done so with the lowest grade-point average, probably 2.0, the minimum. Each student has given a dollar to the anchorman, so as a consolation prize, he starts his tenure as an officer around $1,000 richer. When this happens, cognoscenti turn and explain what is happening to the ignorant; there are rustlings all across the stadium, more applause, and whoops.

When the last company is called ("And now from the thirtieth company!"), we know things are winding up. Gradually we trickle back to our seats. Parents quiet, midshipmen strain forward eagerly on their chairs. The dean ascends the podium, begins to speak. The entire class is declared Bachelors of Science. They have graduated from college.

Some applaud, but clearly they are saving their energy for the big one: a few minutes later, they take the oath as officers; first Marine Corps, about 10 percent of the class, then Navy. The Marines rise from among the mass of seated midshipmen like individual stalks that somehow escaped the threshing machine. They hold their right hands cupped. Do they solemnly swear? They do. And then give "the sound of a Devil Dog": "Yut!" The guttural sound of a mass of males—even though some of the newly commissioned Second Lieutenants are women—hovers in the air for a moment before dying away. Grins split the Marines' faces. For a few moments, they are officers and those sitting next to them are not, like the first of two twins that will always be older than the other. Then it is the turn of the Ensigns-to-be. For this, what seems like the whole block rises in a whoosh, the now-seated Second Lieutenants lost, their moment over.

Graduation and commissioning are two distinct things, though they happen within minutes of each other. The newly minted Navy Ensigns and Marine Corps Second Lieutenants (at Annapolis, people are their ranks, which are capitalized) are jubilant, pounding each other on the back.

They sing the school song, "Navy Blue and Gold." Recently, the Superintendent, our version of the college president, has made the language gender-neutral: "college men" has become "colleges"; "sailor men" has become "sailors brave." The change was denounced by some as high-handed and authoritarian. We heard that some of the male students had been planning on singing it as it had been, as a protest. The Superintendent obviously felt he had to address the opposition during his Graduation Day remarks, reiterating that he needed the class's cooperation in singing the song as amended. That day, his appeals seem to have worked; there is no dissonance at the moments of the altered phrases. The song ends, as always, with a hearty cry of "Beat Army!" This at least has not changed.

The president of the upcoming Senior Class proposes "three cheers for those about to leave us," and the stadium yells "Hip, hip, hooray!" Then his (or theoretically, her) place is taken by the president of the class that has just been commissioned, now an Ensign or Second Lieutenant. This young (wo)man proposes "three cheers for those we leave behind." "Hip, hip, hooray! Hip, hip, hooray!" yells the graduating class. And then the third time, "Hip, hip," and with the final "hooray!" the hats are flung. It takes them several seconds to reach their apogee. This instant is the photographic moment, and squatting photographers capture it on film as it erupts, over their heads, from whence it makes its way to the newspapers, to publicity brochures, and usually to the cover of the Academy catalogue. It is our happiest moment, emblematic of the institution.

At the end of the hat toss, things fall apart. Some covers go astray or fall back onto members of the graduating class and are flung again, so there are a second and then, briefly, a low-energy third wave of hat tosses. Children have been crowding the field and by now are scrambling wildly among the seats, fighting to snag the hats as souvenirs. Frequently the covers are trodden on and stained with grass or mud. The hat toss is a kind of gigantic recycling effort: these new officers will have no further need of their student covers. Little boys may as well have them to play sailor with.

It must seem to those who throw their hats a sort of celestial valorization: though everyone knows the covers fall to earth and are scooped up by scavenging children, the illusion is that it is God Himself who accepts them. After all, our chapel, built in the Beaux-Arts style of the Academy's building boom of the early 1900s, contains a Tiffany window called "the Heavenly Commission," where a newly-minted Ensign is being given his commission by the hand of God protruding from the clouds.

You can buy a miniature replica of this in the Midshipmen Store, as our bookstore and NAVY-emblazoned-clothing store is called. ("Navy" is invariably in capital letters, probably because it looks more substantial. Our teams have no other name, in contrast to Army's teams, which are called "the Black Knights.") Throwing back the covers seems only fair, a small return gift in exchange for the Heavenly Commission. Flung up into the sky, they seem to disappear, the offering accepted. What greater sign of approbation from on high could we ask? Some of the more enterprising of the child scavengers scurry away with their arms full of half a dozen covers and are later heard refusing to share with those who have come away empty-handed. Sometimes the covers fall at the feet of us faculty members in the seats beside the graduating class. If we know some child who wants one, we are not above making one disappear beneath our robes. I have several. Most of us, however, throw them back toward the graduates, or at a scavenger. For us, there is always next year.

With this explosion in a headwear-factory, the graduation ceremony is over. Beaming parents throng the field, standing in clusters to affix to newly minted officers shoulder boards bearing their first stripes; the stripes have to be threaded through loops built into the uniform jackets. We professors make our way as best we can past the rows of wheelchairs, the cables of the television crews, and the graduates. If I pass students I know, I stop and glad-hand with the parents. Usually I make it back to my car having spoken to no one; our military obligation for the day is over, and we can leave.

Sometimes I think: the great machine has, at least for these graduates, finally ground to a halt. Things will never again be so certain for them as they were at Annapolis, nor so predictable. Here their goals were immediate, the punishments for failing to achieve them equally tangible. Things are less clear-cut in the real world. The likelihood is increasingly slim that they will stay in a downsizing Navy, which will spit them out as thirty-year-old ex-lieutenants into a world they have never really lived in, suddenly requiring them to find their own jobs, rent their own apartments, and do their own laundry. Sometimes the adults on the platform are honest and refer to this uncertainty. I wonder if our students are listening?

The hat toss is exhilarating, but it is also melancholy, like the perfect rose Keats wrote about in his "Ode on Melancholy" that expressed decay in its very perfection. The next moment is the beginning of its dissolution. With the covers at their height, there is only one direction for them to go: down in an arc that ends in the grass and dirt. The inevitable letdown that follows an eagerly awaited event seems the more extreme after such a gesture of abandon. The day itself is both culmination and disappointment, mutating almost immediately into reality, with the students changing to shorts and T-shirts to begin the rest of their lives.

We can achieve order, but by definition it is limited in duration and scope. Think of their spotless "choker whites." How brief the time before a scuff sullies the perfection. But while it lasts, how impressive! Like the hat toss, and like the shining uniforms, the students' gleaming youth will never again be so perfect as in this moment. Order isn't unattainable; it just doesn't last.

Smiles

MOST PEOPLE WHO come to Annapolis visit the Naval Academy, whether during Commissioning Week or during the less jubilant times of year. At the vantage point of the "lookout" on Route 450, many stop to visit Maryland's newly created neo-Soviet-style World War II memorial. All plinths and an oversized metal star, it's the little brother of the Soviet monstrosity in East Berlin's Treptow Park; it's set on the slope under a slightly crumbling 1950's concrete terrace. Seen from here, across the Severn River from the Naval Academy, the tidy town of Annapolis takes on the comforting air of a model-railroad setup or a city seen from an airplane: patterns and shapes, comprehensible to the eye in a single visual gulp.

Visitors stand in the sun, leaning against the pebbled concrete balustrade, looking across the river dotted with the white triangles of sailboats to the buildings at the Naval Academy, which are turned by distance into a single strip of horizontal roofs alternating with vertical windows, dwarfed by the massive sky often heavy with the cumulus clouds of a humid Maryland summer. Behind the Academy rise the spires and domes of Annapolis. The closest are the Academy's gold-tipped, greened-bronze chapel, the graceful Georgian lantern of the Maryland State House, and the lower, squarer top of the Colonial-era MacDowell Hall on the campus of St. John's College, which is packed with trees as if the buildings were arising from a verdant fog. Finally the visitors turn and leave, find their cars, and enter the world they have grasped as a whole from afar.

The bridge across the water from the scenic lookout is a soaring, curving, sinuous structure; it had to be built in an odd, twisted shape to avoid the old bridge it replaced, which stood till the day the new one was finished. A vestige of the old bridge still sticks out into the river to be used by fishermen. In the last years of its life, great chunks of cement had fallen off it, exposing the rusted metal of joints. One of my students, a member of the cycling team, was caught in such a growing crack as he tried to cross the bridge with his teammates. The bicycle writhed under him, and he shattered his jaw on the stone-studded innards of the crumbling concrete, or perhaps on the equally crumbling railing—he can't remember; all he knows is that he awoke in the hospital after a week, and spent the next six months in and out of the hospital, having the fragments of his jaw wired and rewired into something approaching normal.

On the great white bridgeheads (a sign tells us this is the "Naval Academy Bridge"), the huge metal seals of the city of

Annapolis have begun to corrode. From the bottom point of their round faces stream fuzzy vertical streaks of green, like a partly finished mono-color drip painting from the 1950's New York School. Once across this bridge, visitors can follow the road to the main gate of the Naval Academy, the one where tourists may drive in.

Or could, until our recent anti-terror measures. Now outside visitors, each of whom must show a picture ID (terrorists don't have such things, apparently), must walk in. Jersey barriers only partly disguised with huge stone flower pedestals block our entrances. When terror alerts change color, there are sniper-nests of sandbags with Marines manning machine guns past the checkpoints. It all reminds me of my time in what was then the walled city of West Berlin, going into the East: *Sie verlassen jetzt den Amerikanischen Sektor.* You are now leaving the American sector.

Yet what tourists see, once they have braved the guards, almost inevitably makes them smile. They see a world that seems almost perfectly ordered: all the students look alike, all look nice, all stay on the paths and don't stray onto the grass, all salute the officers they pass. I'd guess it's the very gung-ho-ness of the students that's most lovable, their sense of purpose—as I heard a tourist say once, the fact that they're "always hotfooting it somewhere," not to mention the fact that they look so "sharp," as midshipmen say. Then there's the attractive architecture, nautical French, the curlicues on the white stone replaced, as the careful looker becomes aware, with anchors, and with dolphins that peer from stonework waves. Our signature buildings are the work of Ernest Flagg at the beginning of the twentieth century—an architect who also created the monumental gentility of Washington, D.C.'s Corcoran Gallery of Art. The grass is immaculate (nobody walks on it), the squirrels pampered and unafraid, and the floral plantings replaced frequently and carefully tended by the groundspeople.

Certainly tourists love looking at midshipmen. It takes the students a while to adjust to this. My plebes sometimes write papers complaining about the way tourists treat them like animals in the zoo, even asking to have their pictures taken with them. ("Come on over here, Mabel, here's a girl one!") I tell them it comes with the territory, and that furthermore, they love it. They consider the idea as if it's novel, but they don't say I'm wrong.

Who wouldn't get a smile out of our students? The average midshipman, typically male (about 16 percent are women), has "taped off" offending specks of dust from his natty close-fitting uniform, stands up tall, calls any tourist "sir" or "ma'am," looks you in the eye, and, if called upon to do so, shakes your hand with a firm grasp. He must pass a physical readiness test (PRT) twice a year, which means he has to stay in shape. He's probably on a team of some sort and works out in the weight room, so his shoulders are as broad and his waist as trim as they are ever going to be. He is by definition clean-shaven and short-haired, and he has in all likelihood been certified before entrance as being Grade A Beef (we allow a certain number of "waivers" for less-than-physically-perfect specimens). He isn't supposed to be dumb, given the heavy load of courses ranging from calculus, physics, and electrical engineering to English literature that he has to master. And when visitors see masses of these students at parades or football games, their chests out and their spines rigid, how can they not burst with pride? This really does seem to be America's finest.

The term "midshipman" comes from those children who, in the British Navy in the eighteenth century, served amidships, shimmying up the rigging and fetching and carrying for the officers. The term, the women insist to me hotly, is a rank, and so can't be made any more gender-neutral than it is. The traditions, ranks, terminology, and even music of the U.S. Navy come pretty much wholesale from the British Royal Navy—though without, the administration hopes, the three things Winston Churchill listed as traditions of the Royal Navy: "rum, buggery, and the lash."

I'd submit that there's no civilian institution in this country—pick any Ivy-level college or university for an example—where the students come near to putting the same kind of smile on a visitor's face. Students at what midshipmen call "real schools" slouch, avoid the gym, binge-drink, chain-smoke, wear caps inside, and never, ever, say "sir" or "ma'am" to a professor. Not to mention that our students aren't—for lack of a better word—sullen, something I remember being in college. Teaching plebes at the Academy—at least when they are at their best—is like tussling with twenty golden retrievers at once. Who wouldn't be exhilarated?

It's not just the visitors who are cheerful. It's the students themselves, at least until they get out of hearing of authority figures. When you ask a midshipman how he or she's doing, the lowest his scale of responses goes is "Outstanding, sir/ma'am." Part of the military life consists of keeping up appearances, putting on a cheery face to keep everyone's motivation high. Or perhaps it's designed to confuse the enemy into thinking that everything is going very well indeed.

I wonder if the tourists would be smiling if they knew that the military, generally speaking, looks down on the civilians they have pledged to defend. I wish I had a dollar for every time I've heard the phrase "civilian scum" here at Annapolis, a taxpayer-supported institution. The midshipmen are told, and most believe, that what they are doing is a higher, purer, better thing than the lives of the people not fortunate enough to live on their side of the Wall that surrounds the Academy. (Once again I think of Berlin.) From the perspective of the Marines, even more demanding and unforgiving of weakness than the Navy, almost all the civilian world is corrupt and soft.

Camp Tecumseh

THE MIDSHIPMEN SOMETIMES call the Academy "Camp Tecumseh," after the chalk-white stone figurehead replica in front of their dormitory, Bancroft Hall, who's referred to as "Tecumseh." By extension, the courtyard of Bancroft Hall, home to all of the Brigade's currently 4,200 students, is called Tecumseh (or T) Court.

Yet the figurehead isn't of Tecumseh, a notably bellicose Native American chief, but of a less-well-known figure from the largely pacific Delaware tribe. This wasn't martial enough for the midshipmen, so they simply rebaptized him. Before football games, he is "war-painted" in garish colors and his plinth festooned with slogans particular to the team he is to lead us to conquer. After the game, whatever the result, the paint and slogans are washed away by a pressure hose and the ground runs colors that disappear into the cracks between the bricks. Before exams, students try to throw pennies into his quiver; for this reason he is known, in a moderately witty pun, or at least one appropriate for a naval institution, as the "god of the C."

It's not just in painting up "Tecumseh" (which might as well be written without the quotation marks; the statue has *become* Tecumseh, or the reverse) that student artistic talent is exhibited. There is a whole culture of drawings and creative slogans at the Naval Academy. Plebes are set early on to making bulletin boards in the hallways of Bancroft Hall. The boards bristle with swooping scarlet airplanes cut from construction paper, like a kindergarten project gone over the deep end into the macabre, and the planes belch construction-paper death while beneath them musclebound G.I.-Joe-type soldiers dressed in pseudo-Medieval garb swing giant swords from the prop-closet of video-game and Dungeons and Dragons combat.

These musclebound heroes, the same ones plebes doodle on their notebooks, continue their combat on behalf of Navy in other places too. For many years, football games were marked by the production of so-called "spirit buttons," large discs with pins on their backs whose designs were chosen by a student-submissions contest. To my jaded eye, some of them looked like thinly disguised rape or sodomy scenes—perhaps in an echo of one of Churchill's "traditions." One year, a gloating Bill the Goat, our mascot, seemed to be ramming the squawking eagle mascot of the opposing team. Another showed a man strapped to a chopping block with a ripped Bill, brandishing an axe, behind him. One midshipman told me this was based on the male-male rape scene in the movie *Pulp Fiction*. I wondered if they were all supposed to be inside jokes among the students: how far could the innuendo go before the adults caught on? Apparently it did go too far, or perhaps my eye wasn't the only jaded one. One whole game's worth of spirit buttons were confiscated as "unprofessional." Then, abruptly and certainly not coincidentally, the spirit buttons were no longer produced. I am left with my collection of greatest hits hung forlornly on the board in my office. I liked their primary colors, their amateurish adolescent drawings and usually mangled metaphors created by alliteration exhorting Navy victory over that weekend's football rival. "Flush the Falcons," said one, showing a Popeye-shaped midshipman with a toilet and a plunger, as well as a hapless bird apparently about to be stuffed down. Some were better: the *Pulp Fiction* one encouraged the team to " 'Get Medieval' on the Knights"— the Black Knights, that is.

I used to get a kick out of seeing the nattiness and general drabness of their uniforms defiled by these oversized, clanking discs. At their "attention on deck," coming to attention as I enter, I'd see (and hear) a classroom of black and white punctuated by an intermittent pattern of bright circles (wearing spirit buttons was encouraged but not mandatory). How ridiculous they seemed, and yet how proud the students were of being able to wear something that wasn't "issue" merely because they chose to.

Of course, their choices were binary: wear it, or don't wear it. Wearing something else in its place wasn't an option. At Annapolis, even allowed deviations from the norm are rigidly controlled. The spirit button, its amateur garishness apparently overlookable, was the only permissible addition to the uniform, further controlled by having only one acceptable placement on the uniform. The students' multicolored textbooks' riotous and undisciplined alternation from red to blue to green and back to blue are tamed when the books are arranged from tallest to shortest. Perhaps a future administration will mandate uniform book covers to eliminate the color divergence. The disordered nature of my own life during my years at Annapolis—disturbed stepchild, hellish marriage, protracted divorce, my brother's death from AIDS—makes me smile ruefully at the Academy's rage for order. If I stay around long enough, I think, they'll be out there starching the blades of grass in the Yard to make them do an "attention on deck."

Bride of Thanatos

DESPITE THE FACT that the Naval Academy is such a shrine of glorious youth and exuberant perfection, it is at the same time a necrophile's dream. The stadium is normally used for football games, a shrine to muscled youth. Yet given that its full name is Navy–Marine Corps Memorial Stadium, it is also a shrine to death in battle. Our graduates jump up and down in ecstasy on Graduation Day under a frieze of battle names: Belleau Wood, Guadalcanal, Corregidor, Da Nang. Across the water on Hospital Point is a cemetery for fallen heroes, now so full that only the deceased of a certain rank can be buried there; lesser once-mortals are cremated and subsequently inhumed in a marble wall that is the single most visible structure on that side of the water to a viewer positioned behind our library. I'm told it's a favorite place for trysts, though being caught isn't recommended.

The single most recognizable building in the Yard is the chapel, where I was married for the first time, to my childhood sweetheart a year after I started at Annapolis, a marriage I now regard as one of the greatest mistakes of my life. Under its nave lies a coffin with a reportedly well-preserved body inside, that of the "Father of the Navy," John Paul ("I have not yet begun to fight") Jones. The reports come from those sent in 1904 to find the long-forgotten body, a sort of nautical saint's relics to put under the church's altar. They rediscovered the coffin under a Parisian street. I remember a childhood trip to the chapel crypt: the shining dark marble, the hushed voices, the funereal black dolphins that arch eternally as they support the black sarcophagus, the click of the Marine's shoes as he marches back and forth. Death, especially clad in ceremonial regalia, makes an effect on the mind of a sensitive child. It's all a gift from France— John Paul Jones, after all, fought the British—a miniature version of the two-story marble and dark metal shrine to Napoleon in the Invalides, as I realized years later.

Many funerals take place in this chapel. I continue teaching while they are going on, but the *thud, thud* of the drum as mourners follow the coffin down the road calls my thoughts away from whatever we are doing in the classrooms, and it distracts the students. As well it ought: though Socrates perhaps went too far in suggesting that life should be spent in preparation for death, young men and women who are in an institution whose purpose is to deal death should, perhaps, reflect on it occasionally. Most likely, they fail to make the connection between the death in bed of an octogenarian and what might befall them now.

It can happen to them, for example, in one of our several swimming pools. Learning to swim is a requirement at Annapolis—no surprise, since these people will spend their careers on the water. Before they can enter their second-class (junior) year, they must swim for forty minutes in their uniform of shirt and long pants. They must also jump from the ten-meter diving platform, arms crossed over their chests like a dead pharaoh. Some balk. One noontime swim I watched as a brawny man and a scrawny woman climbed the ladder, stood at the top, were exhorted by the lieutenant on the ground ("jump NOW"), and then finally turned around and made their way back down the ladder. If they do not manage to jump before the end of the year, they are out.

Since many of our students aspire to be SEALs, the killer divers of the Navy, they try to swim underwater holding their breaths for as long as they can, with or without official permission. Sometimes they overdo it. Every couple of years about a decade ago, a student would fill his lungs with water trying to hold his breath too long. One year, one was fished up from the bottom during a swim exercise and pumped out: he walked away but was rushed only hours later to the hospital, where he died. The authorities clamped down. The signs in the old pool, the charmingly named "Scott Natatorium," now dank and in need of refurbishing, went in a few years' time from nonexistent, to NO SWIMMING WITH LESS [sic] THAN THREE PEOPLE (many discussions ensued over whether that meant two plus one's self or three plus one's self), to NO SWIMMING WITHOUT THE LIFE-GUARD. When I first came, there were no lifeguards. But that also meant that swim times weren't limited to a narrow window

at lunchtime. Now all pools simply forbid: NO SWIMMING UN-
DERWATER.

One of the lunchtime-swim regulars for many years was a
wizened little man, a retiree allowed for that reason to use the
pool at noon, named Tony. I knew his name because I'd hear the
other old men in the locker room—shockingly, to eyes used to
the bodies of twenty-year-old swimmers, exposing their non-
midshipmanlike flesh to get in and out of their clothes—chat-
ting with him. One day I came in to find Tony stretched out on
the tile floor, getting CPR from an Air Force officer.

Tony always wore a midshipman bathing suit, which at the
time was a type of Speedo in blue and gold. (Since then, the
"issue" swimsuit has gotten floppier and longer.) Surprisingly, it
fit him. The combination of his tight but gnarled body and the
snug-fitting, almost glistening student bathing suit was touching as he lay there having life pumped back into him. I noted the
suit again some weeks later: as I was walking into the building,
Tony was being wheeled out, on a gurney, still wearing his
midshipman-issue suit. He had collapsed with his boots on, or
at least his Speedo, in the middle of a lap. He survived to finally
expire two years later in the locker room.

There are deaths outside the pool too. One year, a newly arrived female student dropped dead after only a few weeks: it
turned out she had a defective heart, something neither she nor
her family was aware of. It was, we were told, just one of those
things. Every year a student or two wraps a car around a tree
during spring break. Usually he (it's almost invariably a he) ends
up as ashes in the crematorium wall, and a wave of e-mails com-
memorates his passing. Retiree funerals are typically in the late

morning. The procession, sometimes with the band, sometimes with bagpipes, winds its way down the street in front of my classroom windows, the *boom-boom-boom* of the drums vibrating our chairs.

Memorial Hall, the embalmed heart of Annecropolis, may bring death closer to home. It's on the second floor, up an impressive staircase, behind the rotunda of the Beaux-Arts center of Bancroft Hall (called Mother B by the midshipmen in an unconscious homage to Freud). It's a beautiful high-ceilinged room with elaborate cornices, columns, gleaming parquet floors, and then-Captain Oliver Hazard Perry's flag that says DON'T GIVE UP THE SHIP.

It also contains, in addition to other tattered flags from famous vessels, lists of those midshipmen who have died in various wars and conflicts: young people like themselves who went out to war and "gave their lives" for their country. Standing in the quiet among all these shrines to valor, I think about this phrase, to "give one's life." More likely it was taken from them. Even now, of course, we revert to classical metaphors to express such things: sacrifice upon the altar of the polis. This makes things prettier, as when we enjoin the dead to "rest in peace," though they are not resting, but dead.

And of course the campus, or as we call it in an attempt to suggest its nautical nature, the "Yard," is dotted with monuments to the dead, most of them installed in the early decades of the institution, which was founded on this site though in much less impressive form, in 1845. They exhibit the phallic Victorianism of their time, made more martial by the addition of nonfunctional cannons on the corners. The Tripoli monument outside my window is the most florid, with a Trajan's-column-like center surrounded by simpering white marble angels and a handful of surnames cut into the stone; the column seems undersized for its base. This is the Tripoli of the Marine Corps Hymn, where Marines fought "from the halls of Montezuma to the shores of Tripoli," in nineteenth-century conflicts with Barbary pirates.

Death comes closest to individual midshipmen, I am told, during the "body bag" speech of plebe summer. Fleet sailors arrive in Bancroft Hall one summer day carrying body bags, which the mids touch and heft. A good old-time sermon on the fact that they may see their buddies carried out in such bags, or themselves be carried out, brings most, I have been told, to tears, and makes it clear to them, if only for an instant, that they have not come to this institution in order merely to wear snappy uniforms and parade up and down. Like all of us, however, they soon move on to other things, the minutiae of their daily life finally dominating their landscape like the countless blades of grass through which an ant must maneuver.

One young woman I had as a student had been a Marine before coming to USNA, a "prior," what we call those who have been in the fleet or Marine Corps, a "prior enlisted." She had come to terms with the body bags before. She told of a family friend who asked her on her return from Marine boot camp why she wore two dog tags. Her stock answer, repeated so often she hardly thought about it: "One for the body, one for the bag." The friend burst out crying; my student remembers this as a moment of disjunction of perception between those on the inside and those on the outside.

Death is never very far away, at least in theory, because even the smallest infraction is linked to the death of soldiers in battle. When the students complain about having to do X, Y, or Z, the immediate response is, "In battle, the lives of your men and women will depend on detail!" One of the most common phrases the students hear is a variant of "People die if you do that!" The slightest infraction is immediately magnified, through guilt layered over our students' natural idealism—and there is nothing more idealistic than a plebe at the U.S. Naval Academy—into death for other people. And *then* how will you feel? the institution asks them constantly. The Naval Academy is the ultimate Jewish mother.

Their complaints about the rottenness of their lives are unceasing, so in a way it's good that someone points out to them that their living conditions, though depersonalizing, are nothing compared to, say, the conditions of a platoon of Marines in Iraq, hunched in the rain eating their MREs, sealed Meals Ready to Eat (in interestingly Romance-language word order) and thinking of all those people back at Annapolis they left such a short time before with a roof over their heads and three meals a day served in the cavernous King Hall. But the refrain of "people die if you [fill-in-the-blank]" is so unceasing, it's no wonder the students begin, after some months of hearing it, to roll their eyes.

Like a Nun

PLEBE SUMMER IS the boot-camp period of seven weeks that precedes the fall semester. Like nuns before Vatican II, arriving plebes have their hair cut off: like the civilian clothes they leave behind, this discarded hair is a symbol of the old life that preceded their new one; a reminder that they now belong to a larger unit than they did before, and that they must put aside distractions.

It seems to the onlooker that a conscious effort has been made to render plebes physically insignificant, ugly, and ashamed. The uniforms are the sailor-suits civilians associate with small children and the nineteenth century. Made of synthetics, they trap heat and stink. And plebes are rarely allowed to shower: their choice is between using the precious two minutes to run water over their bodies, or to do one more of the thousand and one things their upperclassmen have demanded of them. So they go stinky, their teeth, they tell me, feeling mossy from lack of contact with a brush.

Those plebes who wear glasses have to wear the thick tortoiseshell frames and lenses created from their prescriptions for plebe summer; by the time they come into my classrooms they are allowed to return to the more fashionable eyewear with which they probably entered. The glasses are functionally affixed to their heads with issue eye-straps. Plebes in gym gear must wear their white socks pulled up to their knees. They seem sexless: this is part of the plan. They are run so hard they lose muscle-weight, not to mention (so I've been told) all trace of sex drive, and the women's breasts dwindle. The women's hair is cut off abruptly at the collar, so that they seem as grotesque in their way as the shorn men do in theirs. The whole lot of them look like a litter of newborn puppies.

On Induction Day ("I-Day" for short), they raise their right hands and swear to uphold the Constitution. Then they are in the Navy. As for what happens after that, in the words of a student in my creative writing course, "The point is to make it perfectly clear that you can never be right."

They are yelled at, "broken down in order to be built up again," taught that they have to trust the person next to them and rely on him or her, subjected to people telling them they are scum and yelling in their face as they spit out memorized passages of the plebe's "Bible," a slim volume called *Reef Points* that fits in the hip pocket of their sailor-suit "whiteworks." Woe betide any plebe who cannot immediately, and with "an upperclass" (the more recent coinage is "a cadre") yelling insults, immediately deliver his or her "rates." Woe betide—the phrase seems particularly apt at Annapolis—any plebe who fails to remember the name of an upperclassman. Woe betide any plebe who fails to "chop" (jog) through the hallways of Bancroft Hall. Woe betide any plebe who hasn't memorized *Reef Points*. Woe betide any plebe who doesn't—well, practically anything. The idea is to find something to yell at them about.

There is the physical side too, PEP (Physical Education Program, which the plebes call the Plebe Extinction Program), with calisthenics in the early a.m. out on the field, and group runs, now limited to three miles. In the last few years, plebe summer has become, by anyone's estimation, less tightly wound. Depending on one's viewpoint, this is either a lamentable crumbling of standards or a bow to reality, a necessary loosening-up. The upperclassmen can no longer touch plebes without asking permission. I think this rule is probably to avoid any charges of sexual harassment of female plebes, an increasingly hot topic, but it also serves to avoid possible injuries—a second-classman poking a plebe in the chest just a bit too hard, for example, or inadvertently pushing him off balance and causing a freak accident. The Academy is not immune to lawsuits, after all, and the standards of the outside world have begun to infiltrate our halls to a greater degree.

Of course, those students who were subject to such discipline taunt the newbies about the unmanly nature of their denatured experience: "I had a *real* plebe summer," each class claims, to annoy the incoming class, in much the same spirit that the final all-male class before the introduction of women in 1976 had engraved in their class rings, according to report, LCWB (Last Class With Balls).

Diluted though it may be, plebe summer is full. Plebes take academic placement tests; learn to sail lasers, the one-person boats that frequently dump them into the sea-nettle-infested waters of the Chesapeake Bay (this teaches them fast, they say); learn to shoot pistols; learn to drill—march in parades, go every-where in step; learn to salute; learn to stand "braced" (it means making double chins against your neck); and learn to call any-thing that moves "sir" or "ma'am." And other things too. One day I was walking down by the seawall during plebe summer and heard a cacophony in a lineup of dumpsters: plebes were in-side, trying to plug holes with chunks of wood while fire hoses sprayed them with water. Clearly they were delighted.

There are five permissible responses from a plebe during plebe summer. These five phrases, all placed in a "sandwich" (both preceded and followed by either "sir" or "ma'am," depend-ing on the sex of their interlocutor), are "Yes" ("Sir, yes, sir!"), "No," "Aye-aye," "I'll find out," and "No excuse." During this time, there is no TV, no Internet, and no music, except for the now-sanitized marching cadences (they're no longer smutty) that repeat over and over, "Two-zero-zero-eight [or whatever the graduation year is], Two-zero-zero-eight, goooooooooooo [drawn out for two counts] NAVY [this at top volume], fight!" The purpose is to create class solidarity, as they also create com-pany solidarity and solidarity with their "swim buddies." During the summer, I hear the plebes being marched around outside my window, being bonded into units greater than the dreaded individual. (Later a Superintendent is to finger "individualism" as one of our great evils; the other is "cynicism," which apparently means anything other than smiley-faced optimism.)

At the end of plebe summer comes parents' weekend, when parents are allowed back to see what's left of their son or daughter. They frequently find an erect, more confident, less childlike young man or woman. And then classes start, and on that first day late in August when I enter the room, they shoot to attention as if spring-loaded, happy to have survived.

What Do We Tell
the Grunts?

SOMETIMES, THE CONNECTION between what we do in the classroom and battle, where they could die, is clearer than at others. Late in 2004 and early in 2005, we are immired in the occupation phase of a real, albeit small war, the second Gulf War. One of my students has some insider knowledge of this. He's a "prior," a Marine who entered Iraq as part of the U.S. Marine forces and found himself, as Vice President Cheney suggested he would be, welcomed as a liberator.

He has a strong negative reaction to one of the books I assigned as part of a unit on Erich Maria Remarque's classic novel about World War I, *All Quiet on the Western Front*. The accompanying text is Chris Hedges' affecting *What Every Person Should Know About War*, which asks a series of dry questions (Will I be afraid in battle? What does it feel like to die?) to make the point that wars affect much more than just the soldiers involved in them, and affect the soldiers more than just on the battlefield. War disrupts the fabric of society in a way that most soldiers on the field cannot imagine.

That battle disrupts soldiers' lives too is Remarque's point—even, perhaps especially, survivors'; the dead are merely dead. His narrator is a young man named Paul who, along with his classmates, has signed up in the fervor of German nationalism largely because of the enthusiasm of their teacher, a certain Kantorek. Now that they are actually involved in the horror of stalemated trench warfare against the British, they despise the older generation and its lies that told them war would be glorious. Under bombardment, they are surrounded by quotidian gruesomeness. They find legs with no torso in a tree; a man is pulverized inches from his friend; horses, wounded in battle, trip over their own entrails and whinny horribly in their pain. Paul all but kills a Frenchman with a knife and then has to spend the night in a shell hole with him while he dies.

My Marine is a plebe, short and wiry. At twenty-three, he is older than almost all of his fellow midshipmen, most of whom he must address as "sir" and "ma'am." He has strong views that he is initially unable to articulate. Moving on from Remarque, which my Marine mistook for a diary by a soldier in battle rather than recognizing it as a novel, we discuss the Hedges in an attempt to answer the question, Are wars nowadays different from the one portrayed by Remarque?

Finally, toward the end of the period, a reaction he has apparently been trying to suppress explodes. "This book," he insists forcefully, unable to remain silent any longer, "is bull!"

"Could you explain that statement?" I ask. He begs off, shaking his head.

After class, lingering for a moment before running to his next class, he opens up. "That's not what I experienced, Sir," he insists.

"Why didn't you say that in class?" I ask.

It seems he wasn't sure he was allowed to disagree. He's been able to do so so infrequently in his life, after all, that he's not very good at what we might call surgical-strike disagreement rather than the carpet bombing of "This book is bull!" He calms down as I assure him that it's okay to disagree with a text, but that the exercise is to identify what specific aspect you disagree with.

I wish my Marine had spoken up in class. He has a point. It's probably true that Hedges, a newspaper war correspondent and divinity-school graduate, didn't want to focus on positive experiences like my Marine's—or those, say, of the American victors in World War II Normandy, men who felt the exhilaration of war along with (or perhaps, in the case of the brief Iraq skirmish, shorn of) its grimness. That would have been a good point to discuss with his less-experienced classmates. But at the same time, he needs to get the point that his experiences, already brief and unrepresentative for the whole Iraq invasion, aren't the whole picture for wars in general. They certainly can't compare to the several years Paul Bäumer, in *All Quiet*, spends at the front.

In the next class period, my student is more talkative. We are still talking about Hedges. "I don't think this book is very motivational," the Marine states flatly. Things that aren't "motivational"—which means adrenaline-pumping, moving you forward—are bad here at Annapolis.

"Why not?" I ask. Others join in.

"Because it doesn't make you want to attack," says one. "It talks about stuff like dying. And women being left without husbands. And orphans."

"Yeah," says another.

"Well," I say. "You may be right. Do all books have to be motivational?"

"For the grunts they do," says the Marine. A grunt is a low-level soldier. He himself was a grunt, a Marine lance corporal, so I accept the term. It's pejorative if applied from the outside but worn by those on the inside as a badge of honor.

"Are all books meant for grunts?" I ask. "You're going to be officers. Should officers have another view of what's going on?"

"Maybe so," admits one.

"I think that's Hedges' point," I say. "That war is more than what takes place on the battlefield."

Again, my Marine is on to something. The gulf between what we do in our English classrooms, or for that matter in the other academic classrooms, and what the midshipmen are asked to do by the military side of the Yard sometimes seems very wide. "Motivational" is, after all, anything that makes you want to charge blindly ahead. For the military, the only permissible direction is forward, except when it's backward: both require decisive action. Decisive action requires good morale. At the Naval Academy, the bottom-line question is always: is X good or bad for morale? If it's bad for morale, it's bad.

Even our language is motivational. Here at Annapolis, we don't decide we were wrong, which would indicate weakness; we "reverse ourselves." It sounds much more volitional. Even apparently passive things, like allowing sleep to overpower us, are reconfigured in the active: here we tell midshipmen to "get some sleep!" Go out and seize it. More generally, the Marine Corps exhorts its members to "Get some!" The "some" refers to anything challenging. No wonder they approve of politicians who act like those toys that roll inexorably across the carpet until they hit a wall, which trips a switch making them scuttle equally purposefully off in the opposite direction.

Hence too the somewhat questionable nature of USNA ethics courses, instituted in a hurry in the wake of massive cheating scandals in the 1990s, and of Academy-wide "Character Development Seminars." I've taught these, and I know how disoriented our students become when I tell them I want discussion and don't care how it turns out. First they set their jaws: I have to be lying to them. Just give us the bottom line, their clenched jaws say to me, and stop the charade. As it begins to dawn on them that I really don't have a bottom line, they become angry, smelling the rank scent of "relativism." It's one of the essential distinctions between liberal and conservative: the currency of conservatism, and hence of the military, is action. The currency of liberalism is talk.

A Visit from the Colonel

EVEN LITERATURE HAS to be motivational. The problem is, what we teach in English departments—what we call "great literature"—rarely is. I sometimes teach Tim O'Brien's short story "The Things They Carried." It has the pedagogical advantage over other stories we read of being about war, a subject of interest to our students. The trouble is, it doesn't seem to encourage action the way they think it ought to. Yet they're not deterred by this. Invariably they begin the discussion telling me it does.

O'Brien focuses on the things that grunts, as well as their single young officer, carried. The things he means are both tangible and intangible: objects, memories, hopes, thought, more objects. The soldiers are described as randomly burning villages, shooting children and old men, taking as a trophy the thumb of a dead adolescent, a VC "soldier," and then going to another place to do it again.

O'Brien focuses on "the things they carry" to suggest that this was not a war about individuals or principles, but about things. Or at least, the things are all that's left to give meaning to what otherwise would be meaningless. The individual grunts are barely sketched, and the lieutenant is left with his adolescent crush on a student that even he ultimately sees is pointless. The things they carry include the amazing toys that appear in the middle of this war zone, such as sparklers for the Fourth of July and colored eggs at Easter, as well as such an inexhaustible supply of armaments that the soldiers blow up their ammunition simply to ditch weight or to amuse themselves.

What my students routinely assure me the story is about, however, is the late-hour remorse of the young Army lieutenant, himself barely older than his men. He blames himself for having inadequately taken care of those in his charge. One of them, who most of the time is high on marijuana, is shot while returning from the latrines. The story gives no evidence that either the officer or the man has been negligent; it's just one of those things. Yet in a fit of somewhat inchoate remorse, the lieutenant vows to become, as midshipmen say, "locked on," apparently so that he can think the war really does make sense, does have meaning; and that he can influence its course, if only in a small way. Yet his resolution rings hollow in the context of the story: he couldn't, O'Brien intimates, have prevented the soldier's death at the hands of a sniper, and being more "motivated" and "locked on," even if he is able to keep up his resolve in the face of a general lack of plan in this war, will have no effect on such things.

My students, however, assure me that this is a motivational story. The lieutenant learns how to be a better officer. The cost of this realization, to be sure, is the death of one of his soldiers, yet some good comes out of this death. They may tell me this because they are new to the military (by the time we get to this story they have been in the Navy only a few months) and are still full of the idealism of plebe summer. Too, I imagine they say it because they are young; it is well known that the young make the best soldiers, because they don't have any sense of the gravity of what they do when they kill another human being. They have to believe, like the young lieutenant in the story, that their personal decisions matter in a war zone, even one as chaotic and ultimately pointless as Vietnam. How could they carry on if they didn't? In some way I'd almost rather they misread the story. I don't know that I want to have the discussion about the real issue it raises: How do you deal with the dawning knowledge that you're killing and in danger of being killed in a war that's lawful but senseless?

Outsiders visit our English-department classrooms with fair frequency. If it's not a colleague writing a report on us for tenure review, or parents coming for the seniors' Parents' Weekend, it's the division director merely circulating to get a sense of what's going on. Our division director is always a Marine colonel. Several years ago it happened that the colonel was visiting on the day I was teaching plebes a D.H. Lawrence short story called "The Blind Man." The eponymous character, named Maurice, has been blinded in the Great War (World War I) and has returned home to his wife and farm. He's morbidly self-conscious about the disfigurement of his face, and prone to fits of depression. His pregnant wife frequently feels as if his dark moods are too much for her. The adjectives Lawrence uses to describe Maurice link him with the darkness and with the outdoors, as well as with the large animals of the barn, and with trees: he's slow and not, it seems, very bright. But he's large, and he's strong, and he's very physical. His wife Isabel is much more clever. She wrote, we are told, book reviews in her youth, and she seems happier in the lighted spaces of the house than outside in the dark with the cows.

Enter the third member of the triangle, named Bertie. Bertie is a distant cousin of Isabel's, Scottish like her (the blind man is English), very artsy, a fast talker and a successful barrister, clever, but as small and physically slight as the blind man is large and ponderous. He's Maurice's polar opposite. He is also, as Lawrence puts it coyly, "neuter." Many commentators have said that Lawrence is willing to go up to the point just before saying that a character is gay but then backs off, as for example in what seems to most commentators the lesbian fable "The Fox" or the homoerotic sadomasochism of "The Prussian Officer." So perhaps neuter means gay. On the other hand, it may simply mean completely aphysical, which by itself presents a strong contrast to Maurice's physicality.

Unsurprisingly, given the contrasting natures of the two men, Maurice had discouraged visits from Bertie in the early years of his marriage, before he was blinded. He would logically have sensed competition for his wife's attention, knowing that he himself could not keep up with her mentally and that Bertie could. He would also probably have felt the revulsion of the very physical man for the too-cerebral one, even if he had been unable to identify its source. Now, however, with no other male friends and no living beings outside his wife save the cows, Maurice welcomes Bertie's unexpected note to Isabel that is the impetus for the story, and he suggests she invite him to visit.

The visit goes—predictably—badly. The table conversation is strained. Unable to stand it any longer, Maurice finally excuses himself on the grounds that he has to look after the cows. Feeling after a time that he has been out too long, Isabel sends Bertie to fetch him. It is here, in the near-darkness of the barn, among the cows to which Maurice is compared and that he feels to be his friends, that the central encounter of the story takes place.

A major source of Maurice's depression, it seems, has been his inability to get an objective answer from Isabel as to what his scar looks like. As the dutiful wife, she would of course say that it looked fine; or perhaps, that whatever it looked like could not matter to her. Ultimately, someone who saw Maurice objectively and who could speak plainly to him would be necessary to give him what he wants, reassurance that life could after all go on. Being able to speak of the scar with another man would render it merely another topic of conversation. Maurice seizes upon Bertie's presence to ask him to be that objective male. There in the barn, Maurice suddenly wants to speak to Bertie about his scar.

Bertie is honest with Maurice. He says that it is horrible. This is in fact a good thing for Maurice to hear: he's suspected it, and hearing it is the first step toward Maurice's acceptance of the way things are. Then the last Rubicon is crossed: Maurice wants Bertie to touch the scar. If another man can touch it and live, it can't be so bad. Maurice would be cured of his depression, we are sure. It turns out that the better is the enemy of the good. If Maurice had stopped at words, he might have made some progress. As it is, he ruins everything.

Would that the fates had sent Maurice a man as physical as himself, who could have plunged his fingers into Maurice's sockets and laughed good-naturedly, or made a joke, or rough-housed with him, the universal male bonding medium. Instead, the fates sent him the only other male in Isabel's universe, a man who is not even commonly physical, but quite abnormally without physicality in a way that not one man in a thousand (or more) is. Or perhaps Bertie really is gay and unable to admit this; certainly that would make him a less exotic flower.

Bertie is so overwhelmed by the larger man, who is at his ease among the cows in the darkness of the barn, that he does touch the scar, horrified though he is. Maurice then moves to the next step in what he thinks is their bonding process. He asks permission to run his huge hands over Bertie's own slight features by way of gathering information: he wants to touch this man who seems on the way to saving him from the bottomless pit of his own self-pity. Bertie is too cowed and horrified to refuse. The vocabulary Lawrence uses is one of sexual encounter, ultimately rape: Maurice's hand is described as "naked" (aren't hands usually so?); and the hand "takes" Bertie. Certainly Bertie's reaction is one of someone who has been raped: he feels invaded, devastated, like "a mollusk whose shell has been broken."

Poor Maurice: he thinks he's become friends with Bertie, and he's so unable to read cues (that perhaps he simply cannot see), he thinks Bertie has become friends with him as well. Maurice hurries Bertie into the light to announce to Isabel that he has finally found a friend. It would mean he was saved. Isabel, being quick-witted and not blind, looks at Maurice's beaming visage, and Bertie's sour and unhappy one, and sees at once that he has not. She does not know what to say.

The visiting Marine colonel, however, did. He'd had the text for two days, had read it carefully, and was happy to share his conclusions. He announced that this was a story of a man, Maurice, who had identified a threat to his family and neutralized it. He had reestablished control. For the colonel, the story had a happy end: one man had excluded the other, annihilated him intentionally. For Lawrence, by contrast, the story has an unhappy end: one man excludes the other, annihilates him unintentionally when he really just wants a friend and equal.

The idea that a man could annihilate another without having meant to was clearly one that hadn't occurred to our colonel; the depressing end of Maurice, now alone with his pregnant wife after Bertie has left, was not something he could entertain. Or was his misreading, which it clearly was, merely the result of his unfamiliarity with stories that ended badly, as most in literature do?

If a student had offered what was so clearly a misreading of the story, I would have asked for justification and tried to show how much of the evidence seems to speak against his conclusions. With the colonel, by contrast, I only smiled. Assuming that what we were doing in "his" English department had to be useful, the colonel would inevitably look for a reading, no matter how unjustified, that gave a "how-to" lesson. I could imagine his reaction if I had insisted that this was a story that ended badly, with something other than the reestablishment of male control. What would be the point, I can imagine him asking indignantly, of a story that ends badly? Where is the moral? The role model? Why should we emphasize failures?

Very few if any of the works we read in class, I realized, contain role models. Very few are motivational. The war novels we read in class, such as *All Quiet on the Western Front*, are not stories of heroism to rally the troops; instead they show the waste and pointlessness of war. The novels about marriage that we read, such as *Madame Bovary*, show us that marriage frequently not only solves nothing, but makes matters much worse. Even poetry aims for a realization in the reader that we can't have it all. The take-home point of Keats's "Ode on a Grecian Urn," which I read every year with plebes, is that we humans are caught between a rock and a hard place with our desires. They're necessary to keep us moving. But we do not, save in an almost trivial, momentary sense, ever achieve them: once we do achieve our goals, they are no longer goals, and we must find new ones. They slip from us like wraiths.

This, I am now no longer surprised to discover, is not what our idealistic students want to hear. They want to hear that war is worth it, that marriage is the ideal state, and that we can attain, in every sense, what we set out to get. The same is true, I believe, for the officers who lead them, who as a result are suspicious of the goings-on in the English department—and with good cause, when it's seen from their point of view. Literature professors would say that telling my students what they want to hear would be to tell lies. But so what? Even the military would probably admit, in an unguarded moment, that what they say (war is worth it, we can achieve our goals) isn't an accurate description of the world. Rather, what we say, for the military, is less a mirror of the world than part of an interaction with it. Saying that we are "outstanding" when we aren't is a way of bluffing the enemy, and of cementing the bonds with those Inside. Saber rattling is meant to scare off others, not accurately reflect our capabilities.

Herndon

IT'S PARADOXICAL, IF ultimately explicable, that the military is so steeped in a culture of violent death—the ultimate acknowledgment that things can go very wrong—and at the same time so resistant to the way literature points this out. This embrace of the pomp of commemorating death, including the importance given to "full military honors" for the dead and "paying respects," comes from an attempt to control something that's gone out of control, if only after the fact. If we embrace it, we make it ours.

It would be far more upsetting to acknowledge that things can still go out of control in this way even now, as we speak; not merely in the past tense, where we can mourn it, but in the present and future. Or worse, to acknowledge that this lack of control is more typical of our lives than is control. We might think the military would want great literature commiserating with them, saying, Brother, I know it's all a crapshoot. Yet when literature tries to say, I feel your pain at the meaninglessness of it all, the military repulses them: Life isn't a crapshoot! It has meaning! You are the master of your own destiny! The military has dealt with the lack of control in its own way, by embalming it in pomp; the issue is closed and may not be reopened.

For this same reason, the military never accepts that those demonstrating in the street against involvement in a war have the best interests of the troops, among other people, at heart. To the military, the suddenly ubiquitous plastic pretend ribbons magnetized to car bodies that encourage us to "Support the Troops" mean: cheer at their victory in battle. Supporting the troops can never mean: bring them home alive so they don't come home in body bags. The military defends their right to die.

When you die, you get a monument. In the Yard, the single most famous monument to the dead is associated most fundamentally with plebes, though at the end of their plebe year, rather than at the beginning. The simple gray obelisk is known as "Herndon," the single name carved into its base. It is a memorial to a ship captain of that name—though this information is found only in the mental memory files of a thousand plebes and in the history books. (A date floats halfway up the other side: September 12, 1857.) And the ceremony that marks the end of their plebe year takes its name from the obelisk. Ask any plebe, sometime after March, "How many days until Herndon?" and he or she will be able to tell you instantly.

For Herndon (the ceremony), Herndon (the monument) is

smeared with several hundred pounds of lard the night before. A plebe summer cap, called a "dixie cup" because of the way it looks, is placed on the top. At the sound of a cannon at 1330 (military time is marked on a 24-hour clock and without the usual colon) on a day shortly before graduation, the entire plebe class tears out of Bancroft Hall and runs headlong between ropes set up to keep them off the grass and away from the tourists, many of whom have set up lawn chairs hours before to get a good spot from which to enjoy the festivities. In recent years, probably out of a fear of injury, the energy level of the ceremony has been radically reduced, the class having been told to remove its shoes and walk, not run, to the obelisk. This is the kinder, gentler Naval Academy we are constructing in the new millennium.

All the plebes are dressed in PE gear, which is a "blue-rim" white T-shirt and blue shorts that read USNA; women wear bathing suits underneath. Within seconds, at least until recent years, the fastest male runners are at the shining white monument, stripping off their T-shirts and using them to wipe away as much of the white fat as they can. Soon all the boys are shirtless, the better to enjoy the fun. (At present, not only has the energy level been reduced, but apparently we now object to unclothed male torsos in public: shirts were kept on in 2004.) The grease adheres to the marble surface and keeps things interesting even when the stone is no longer snow-white with lard but merely shiny gray.

The front-runners are followed seconds later by the next wave of plebes, who bunch around the monument's base and, for the next several hours, surge, pile, and make futile efforts to reach the top. During this time they step on each other's faces and shoulders in their efforts to pile high enough that one person (who has always been a male rather than a female) can reach up and remove the dixie cup before replacing it with an upperclassman's cap. Seen through time-lapse photography, the accomplishment of this feat would look like waves along a seashore bunching up and then being dragged back out, a crystal structure made of bodies collecting and rising higher, then collapsing again.

When the cannon sounds to mark the successful placement of an upperclass cap on the tip of the obelisk, the men and women at its base are no longer plebes. In practical terms, this means that they cannot any longer be made to perform chow calls (the high-speed repetition of the day's menu so fast that they are incomprehensible while standing at attention before an upperclassman's door), learn "rates" (reams of technical knowledge that must be memorized daily), or "chop" down the hallways of Bancroft Hall (jog rather than walk), punctuating each sharply turned corner with a hearty "Beat Army, sir," or "Go Navy, sir." They are, in short, mercifully no longer the playthings of the upperclassmen. Soon they will themselves be the upperclassmen who play with the next year's plebes, the waves of bodies that determined the rhythm of their Herndon climb functioning like a metaphor for their own arrival on these shores, thrown up, dragged back by the tide, and then thrown up again, only finally to be gone, leaving place for other generations, other waves.

Sometimes, walking the halls of the athletic buildings between the weight room and the bathroom, or on the way out from the pool, I am struck by a sense of being dragged out to sea by this generational undertow. I stop before the pictures of, say, the football team from 1898. The pictures are sepia. The midshipmen are smaller than football players of the late twentieth and early twenty-first centuries, and they wear what seem to us to be rudimentary helmets. They are otherwise indistinguishable from my students, the midshipmen of today. All are short-haired, fresh-faced, square-jawed, staring expressionlessly at the camera; and all are dead, dragged away by time if not by the violent conflicts they were trained to fight.

Sometimes the pathos of these long-dead midshipmen once so strong of limb calls up echoes—as if torn by the wind and waves—of T.S. Eliot's "Death by Water" from *The Waste Land*: remember Johnny, who was once as strong and tall as you; the current picks his bones in whispers. A plaque in the pool where I swim laps dedicates the "timing device" to a certain lieutenant, whose picture as a midshipman hangs nearby, an All-American swimmer shot down in Vietnam only a half dozen years after his graduation. In his SDBs—Service Dress Blues, the doubled-breasted black suit the Navy insists on calling "navy blue"—and sporting his self-confident midshipman smile, he looks like dozens of the students whom I have left only minutes before. Even the timing device has in a sense died and been replaced by an improvement. In the early 1970s, it must have been a clock; now it has transmuted to a rectangular box in which right-angle scarlet bars form digital minutes and seconds, and it is attached to the outlet by a long cord that ends by the water fountains.

But that, of course, is what my students are learning: that they exist as part of a larger whole. They individually are expendable; the only thing that matters is the mission. And so they flow through the halls of this institution, leaving only to serve, grow old, and die. Some are brought here again—for burial in our cemetery on Hospital Point across the creek from Sampson Hall, where we sit studying, say, Modernism, measuring out our days in coffee spoons, aware from within our over-cooled buildings of the thud of the funeral procession outside our walls.

Sometimes I run into my students the evening after Herndon. The grease and sweat have been showered and scrubbed away, and they are wearing spotless summer whites, but many sport bruises and gashes from someone's foot or fingers. They seem as proud of these minor injuries as nineteenth-century German students were of their dueling scars. They are, at any rate, happy not to be plebes.

Gate Guards

ON ENTERING THE gate near Herndon, and next to Sampson Hall, home of the Academy's English and history departments, I stop to let the Marine acknowledge my Department of Defense sticker and my proffered ID card with a wave of his left hand. We have had these impressive-looking Marines at our gates for only a few years; they lend an air of adventure to entering and exiting here. In earlier, less-tense times, people could walk in unchallenged, despite the Marines. And though one gate was designated for visitors, even people unconnected with the Academy could drive in at any entrance if they could name a specific destination in the Yard.

The Marines come from the barracks across the river. Sometimes I see them running in groups in the early morning, in their dirty-green T-shirts and shorts and their black combat boots, sweat-drenched muscular skinheads with the man in the front of the platoon carrying a guide-on flag. I'd think the front man's job was the toughest, with only one arm free to swing because of the flag. But those boots make it hard for all of them; to prepare themselves for the Corps, many of our students go jogging in such boots by the seawall, packs on their backs for extra weight.

Before the Marines arrived to impress the public and now, at least in theory, to stop terrorists, the gates were manned by overweight, middle-aged Department of Defense policemen, considerably less imposing physical specimens, whom we still see in their squad cars giving chase to automobiles that exceed the unforgivingly low posted speed limits. In my first year at the Academy, I got a speeding ticket from one of these policemen, not having understood that even at midnight, cars are supposed to crawl along the deserted roads. With no nod to the fact that I was a faculty member, no warning not to do it again, sir, I was curtly handed a ticket directly payable to a Baltimore civilian court. Coming soon after I'd been in a fender-bender, this ticket upset my insurance company, which tried desperately to drop me and could only be dissuaded by my telling them I had been living for two years in Rwanda. They took this to mean that I had acquired bad driving habits or forgotten good ones altogether, and they relented.

Perhaps for this reason, I listen with glee when my students tell me of outrunning the "jimmy-legs" (for so these DoD police are still called by the midshipmen in pejorative Academy seatalk) when they return illicitly at night by jumping over the Wall, that leftover bit of Cold War mentality that girds our campus and separates it from the town of Annapolis. In the mid-1990s, the Wall was refurbished along King George Street. As part of the renovation, the bricks were completely torn down and replaced with a chain-link fence. During this process, the backs of the officer housing, normally hidden to the street, were exposed, and they were oddly touching with their so-ordinary gardening tools, piled-up lawn chairs, and trash suddenly visible, like underparts usually hidden but now left to dangle in the air.

The newest wrinkle on the jimmy-legs is that they are not to be called "jimmy-legs" any more, as part of the campaign for mutual respect that gained official sanction at the Academy in the 1990s, a campaign pursued with all the sanctimony of the recently baptized. Some would call this alteration of taxonomy overt political correctness on the Academy's part in response to its blatant incorrectness; headline-grabbing scandals were rife in the early 1990s, ranging from our wholesale cheating scandal, to a female mid being found handcuffed to a urinal, to a chaplain who exposed himself at the Annapolis Mall. This is the kind of self-imposed overreaction to which the Navy seems congenitally prone.

As a result of this swinging of the pendulum, we civilian faculty had to sit through mandatory "sexual harassment training" (as if we needed to be taught how to do it), involving lamentably bad films showing actions we couldn't imagine anyone, much less ourselves, engaging in. We sign in to prove that we have attended, and we are certified to be harassment-aware. Those who run the Academy can report to their overseers that they have dealt with the problem, because everyone has attended the training.

This, we perhaps overly smug PhDs observed to ourselves as we sat in darkened classrooms at lunch hour looking at our watches, was brought to us by first cousins of the men responsible for the infamous 1991 Tailhook convention of aviators at which female officers were forced to run a gauntlet of male gropers. (A tailhook, from which the club takes its name, is the hook on the back of a plane that, as the plane lands on an aircraft carrier, is snagged by a cable that keeps it on the carrier's deck.) This one convention forever sullied the reputation of this long-standing aviators' club. No proselytizer like a convert.

Polder

THE ACADEMY SITS in cramped, well-manicured splendor, pressed up against the city of Annapolis. Expansion in that direction—once expansion became inevitable—was clearly impossible. To get more land, the Academy therefore turned to the practice of taking great chunks out of the Severn River and the Bay, creating polder, as in much of Holland, by filling the riverbed in with subaqueous tree trunks and dirt. From the air, the playing fields and structures built upon them on our campus's watery edges look like square terraces of a building jutting out from the more solid walls. This practice, however, has stopped, ecological consciousness having triumphed, not to mention the fact that soon we would be like Venice, built on pilings. Many of the newer buildings are. Academy lore has it that the library, built on landfill, is sinking, the engineers who made its calculations having forgotten that the weight of the books in the building would constantly increase. I have heard that this story is apocryphal, but I like it nonetheless.

Like Venice, however, the Academy is at least an institution—fittingly, it seems—wedded to the sea. The gym where I used to work out, the one that houses Scott Natatorium, started life as a boathouse with a hollow, watery core; the boats maneuvered in the area where students now hoist weights. Sometimes I look up from the gym I now frequent (a newer one, in a campus full of gyms) to the momentarily puzzling sight of a person gliding by beyond the seawall—standing on a boat, I realize a moment later—or the more easily identifiable sails that jump from window to window as they transit across my view, entering or exiting the harbor.

During Hurricane Isabel in 2003, millions of dollars of damage was sustained by the Academy as a tsunami of river water washed into the ground-level laboratories and then flowed through the passageways of the linked buildings across the Yard. In my own building, Sampson Hall, many hundreds of yards from the seawall, the water stood nearly two feet deep and took out the entire ground floor's walls, carpets, and computers. It was the Annapolis equivalent of the Venetian curse of *aqua alta,* when the lagoon floods the streets and squares of that eternally decaying city and people walk about in rubber boots on the wooden sidewalks.

But most of the time, the water merely surrounds us, it does not enter us. Someone coming onto the Yard from the town is immediately surrounded by Flagg's ornate white brick buildings with their green copper roofs, their Athenian or Michelange-

lesque decorations (the edges of the roofs sport triangular Grecian grotesques, and Mahan Hall's pediment echoes the "Night"
and "Day" of the Medici chapel), and by the starker but harmo-
nious science buildings, additions from the 1970s.

The Naval Academy began life in 1845, on the site of old
Fort Severn, where the Severn River joins Chesapeake Bay.
During the Civil War, the Academy, then behind Confederate
lines, was moved to a large, genteel house with a wraparound
porch in downtown Newport, Rhode Island, where today a sign
proudly informs the visitor of this fact, and only later was moved
back. Yet there is no building on our campus dating from 1845.
The oldest structures are from much later in the century,
two unprepossessing white-painted brick structures flanking
Gate 3. One of them serves as the guardhouse for the Marines,
and the other as the public toilets.

Bone Ships

HERNDON IS IN front of Preble Hall, the U.S. Naval Academy Museum, which in turn is next to the building housing the English and history departments, Sampson Hall. The museum's most popular exhibit consists of the many glass cases of impossibly detailed model ships, tiny versions of great objects, protected by glass against which the visitor can press his or her nose in rapt attention, as if the reduction of huge structures that dwarf us tiny humans to a size we can pick up would allow us to control and understand them. Some of these model ships are made of hundreds of tiny carved, painstakingly assembled panels of animal bones, laboriously fashioned by French prisoners of war incarcerated aboard English vessels during the Napoleonic wars. They are marvels of craftsmanship, displayed behind glass and under spotlights, mute testimony to the paradox of mortality—that of the animals eaten, of course, and of the men who left behind these painfully minute testimonials to the futility of human striving: prison work-therapy, inward emigration as a response to enforced, involuntary immobility. What would those prisoners have thought if they were told that the fruits of their boredom would outlive them by so long, and be so treasured?

My own favorite part of Preble Hall, good for filling empty afternoons, is the historical section, with lithographs and even a model of the Naval School (such as it was) in 1845, as well as at various intermediate stages between then and now. None of these earlier archetypes of the Academy looks even remotely like the buildings that define so much of my day. Good Romantic that I sometimes am, I think of photographs of European or Japanese cities that have gone through a number of violent changes since the beginning of the century: the casual visitor sees only the anonymous newer buildings and has no idea of all the others that have stood on these sites, each era's Academy ripped away before the violent birth of its successor.

Nothing is forever. Those of us who live in societies that change slowly lose a sense of this; certainly the U.S. Naval Academy, with its emphasis on tradition, encourages one to believe that things never alter, or only in a logical, slow, accretive way. Seeing all of these images arranged together against one wall in Preble Hall so that they flicker like a stroboscope allows us to understand that this is not so.

Along another wall are a ragged gaggle of souvenirs—an African statue, an idol from Tonga—brought back in more innocent eras by those who, with ships, went places where few had gone before. I am charmed by this evidence of a world Outside that no longer exists—no longer, that is, as Outside. It is as if these little wooden statues contained all the wonder and adventure of joining the Navy and seeing the world, a wonder that was possible only in an era of a smaller world and a more absolute Outside.

In one showcase are pictures of long-dead "color girls," ancestors of those whose pictures appear below them in a showcase devoted to their lore. Color girls were, and are, girlfriends or female relatives of the commander of that company picked, each spring, as the highest-ranked in military and academic endeavors of the Brigade's companies. The Color Parade is an integral part of the pageantry of Commissioning Week.

Now the institution of the color girl itself is under attack, as some of the female midshipmen express their understandable resentment at having to stand on the field at attention in their boiled-wool suits while a frilly young thing in bows and ribbons and wearing a floppy hat is paraded about as the symbol of "real" femininity, a lust-object for hundreds of immobile, rigid young men clutching their parade rifles. And what will happen if the commander of the color company is a woman? Will a color boy be flown in, given a suit and a pair of cufflinks, and paraded about the field? Or will "chance" simply have it that a female-commanded company is never chosen?

Pageantry

DURING THE WEEK, students hurry to classes across the Yard, so that for a period of ten minutes every hour the sanctioned brick arteries leading to the classroom buildings from Mother B are clogged, as after a sudden rainfall, with a stream of black-clad bodies wearing white caps; then, for the next fifty minutes, the dominion of the pampered squirrels is reestablished, with the sun shining on the hints of late-winter green in the grass—and then once again the deluge, producing an alternation of utter quiet with frenetic activity that becomes irregular only around lunchtime, when the stream is more strung out and goes in the other direction, toward noon-meal formation in the encircling arms of Mother B, or when classes are let out a few minutes early by a generous professor. Those few minutes are in fact a precious gift: minutes to midshipmen are the equivalent of

hours to other students, for a minute can mean the difference
between shoes properly shined and a demerit, the difference between a room acceptably ordered and a black mark. Midshipmen have to change uniforms frequently. As plebes, they have
uniform races to see which company can get out of one uniform
and into another the quickest. Changing clothes in record time
is a much-prized skill at Annapolis.

The torrent of uniforms is black and white only during the
winter. On a certain date—they are always able to tell me,
though I never remember—the dark suits are abruptly wiped
away one morning by open-necked dark shirts that themselves,
at a specific date only weeks later, turn white. The visual effect,
in fact, produced by these uniform changes on someone looking
at the Yard over a period of seasons is similar to that produced by
those ranks of fans who, at a football game or political rally, hold
up cards that spell or form something; then they turn them over
and in an instant a sea of one color becomes a sea of another.
When this happens, a slightly different cast is thrown over the
Yard, like a change in lighting on a stage, and just as unpredictable. The changes are only loosely correlated to the actual
change of weather; the appropriate uniforms are determined
well in advance and by people deciding for other reasons than
those of midshipman comfort—so that sometimes there is a period of days or weeks where the students shiver in their short
sleeves, or sweat in their suits. I think sometimes of the cherry-
blossom festival in Washington, D. C., that, as often as not,
takes place when the blossoms are still tight in bud, or have long
since bloomed and are nothing but a memory.

If the tourists come as part of what I think of as a "ye olde"

Colonial Annapolis tour, they walk in following a woman wearing eighteenth-century garb including a big sun hat and carrying a basket in lieu of a more modern purse, or a man in a tricorn and knee stockings. If they have come on their own, checking in at the Armel-Leftwich visitor center built onto the Field House some years back, they will be following a woman (more rarely a man) dressed in blue and gold who explains things to them. Here is Bancroft Hall, the "largest dormitory in the world." Here is Herndon. Here is the museum with the bone ships.

Many tourists come for noon-meal formation. They toe up to the line painted across the bricks at the opening of T-Court before Bancroft Hall. Only a tiny fraction of the midshipmen can fit into T-Court's tight embrace, and the other companies do their musters inside the building, or behind it—as presumably all could do, if it weren't for the fact that the middle of the day would then lack anything for the visitors to see. In fact, Bancroft Hall is not a single building at all, though admitting this would challenge the tour guides' claim that it's the "world's largest dormitory." Instead, it's a core onto which symmetrical wings were added as the Brigade grew in size, then more wings added to those; behind it are separate outlying buildings divided by a road and connected to the mother ship only by aerial walkways that provide more living space, and yet are still counted as part of the "same building."

At a noon-meal formation, the part for the tourists, the "show" companies that do fit into T-Court form phalanxes and wait, along with the tourists. At 1210, a triangle of the Brigade staff—students picked to lead the student body, and who are themselves led by the Brigade Commander—march in formation down the steps. The midshipmen in ranks come to attention. The drums of the musicians accompanying the Brigade Staff down the steps keep the beat, and the small band following them plays. Company officers give their report ("All present or accounted for, sir/ma'am,"), which is relayed up the chain. Eventually the triangle of Brigade Commander and his or her adjutants reverses its direction and disappears up the steps; the band plays "Anchors Aweigh" and the Marine Corps hymn. The midshipmen file off; the show is over. This happens daily, barring cold or inclement weather.

The most public, and most picturesque, of the midshipman rituals in a campus defined by ritual and pageantry are their parades, of which the most colorful is Commissioning Week's Color Parade ("color" refers to the flag). Seeing even the less festive parades requires some advance planning because they typically take place only on Wednesday afternoons in the spring and fall, and very occasionally on Fridays. In the parade season, I am scrupulous about getting out of my office before my car is blocked by marching students.

The parades beg to be compared to theatrical performances or dance programs. Ushers—plebes, officially Midshipmen Fourth Class; seniors are Midshipmen First Class, or "firsties"—show spectators to their seats ("Bleachers on either side, sir") and hand out programs. A voice as disembodied as that which informs us in a theater that Miss X is indisposed and that we may not take photographs comes over a public-address system for announcements. Photographs are encouraged here. There are always dignitaries present too, sitting in the equivalent of the presidential box in a theater. Music is provided not from an orchestra pit but by the Academy Band. And if the brilliantly green and absolutely flat grass of Worden Field isn't a stage, it is certainly treated with the care befitting one by the grounds crew. It is so smooth it glistens. There are even critics: officers with clipboards grading each company to see which one will become the color company next year and carry the flag.

Aside from the entrance and exit (fully half of the time), the prime step is standing: stillness as action, underlined by the sheer mass of performers, the vast potential for chaos in all these bodies that are being so carefully controlled. Even the entrance and exit seem, in contrast to this standing, relentless and somehow pure motion—measured, vast, and yet ultimately touching because so completely held in check. The viewer senses pure concentration on the field, like the brow-furrowing attempt to put a little piece in a machine just *there*: all the control is exercised in damping down, in an act of distillation rather than expansion or dilution. Commands are relayed across the field in faraway shouts that produce, all at once, a massive and yet infinitesimal alteration in the companies. Thousands of white-gloved hands flick from waists to sides; we see a flutter of black as the performers separate one leg from the other to stand at parade rest. Thousands of hands slap in unison on their rifles.

A parade at Annapolis, despite the fact that some of our students are women, is still a predominantly male show, a display of flagrantly masculine postures: squared shoulders, thrown-out chests. Yet there is usually at least one woman among the three company leaders who march in a triangle before the square formations of midshipmen behind them; women's steps, being shorter than those of the almost perfectly unison men, provide a kind of rustling visual counterpoint to the otherwise seamless flow. (The male students complain that the females are overrepresented, for political reasons, in these front-and-center slots.) These minor undercurrents aside, this is about unanimity, breathless in its power. The crowd goes wild.

The reality up close doesn't match the cumulative appearance of order seen from the stands. It is the same with the Benday dots of the hat-toss picture: closer isn't better. Tourists should be glad they're up in the stands. When the command "pass in review" comes, the midshipmen are usually murmuring "piss in your shoe." Under their so-natty jackets, many are wearing torn T-shirts (they tell me so, and sometimes they show me with a grin). Their shoes frequently have holes in the soles ("Sir, it takes so long to get them back from the cobbler!"). Their rifles are filled with lead. And who knows what they're thinking? I do: most of them despise drill.

In the spring, as the weather warms, a few of them always faint from standing still so long in the wool jackets they were fitted for as plebes and that many have outgrown, bulking up over four years in weight-workouts or of overeating at the "fat boy" table in King Hall, the cafeteria where all 4,000-plus of them sit down to consume huge quantities of food in a few minutes and then are gone like locusts, leaving a huge cleanup job for the staff. As a result, ambulances with paramedics stand ready at each parade, and they take three of our available parking spaces by the side of Worden Field on parade Wednesdays. During the parade, students on the sailing team, excused from drill, sail the boats back and forth on the Severn beyond, their colorful spinnaker sails bellied out, to provide a visual backdrop.

But it is the fall parades that seem somehow more beautiful, the Academy caught in the contrast of the beginning of the academic year and the end of the calendar one, or at least the end of summer. It is a time of paradox, of sweetness mixed with regret, of death being born out of life. By the side of the field are the ginkgo trees that in autumn drop the sweetish, rotten fruit that I try to step around on my way to my car. People look upward to catch the suddenly weaker sun on their faces. It feels like the beginning of the end, and yet the students are new, and anything seems possible.

It is for this reason that when I close my eyes far away from Annapolis, I see it in the autumn, this transition time between summer and winter, the arrival of new students and the traces in memory of those who have so recently gone, now serving on ships, running obstacle courses for the Marine Corps down in Quantico, or studying for a specialty school, having experienced what they call the "biggest demotion in the Navy," the step from Midshipman First Class at the U.S. Naval Academy to a mere Ensign in the real Navy, or Second Lieutenant in the Marine Corps. No wonder they look back with such nostalgia at their "four years by the Bay."

Athens vs. Sparta

PRIOR TO THE Vietnam era, the academic curriculum at Annapolis was the same for all midshipmen; everyone shouldered the same engineering-heavy course load. A more diversified curriculum—which necessitated the construction of the library that apparently is not sinking—whose purpose was to make us a more attractive institution to the increasingly antimilitary population, allowed majoring in individual subjects, including four nontechnical ones: English, history, political science, and economics. Yet even English majors take a heavy base of core courses in such subjects as "calc" (calculus), "diffy-Q" (differential equations), "wires" (electrical engineering), physics (no short form), and "weps" (weapons). English majors may be reading poetry, but it's only as a single course in a huge meal.

The debate continues to rage concerning what proportion of

the class should be allowed to major in nontechnical subjects. The proponents of Admiral Hyman Rickover's "nuclear Navy" insist that anything above 20 percent of the class is a "hit" that the Navy will not survive—the presupposition being that this percentage will be dead weight, or at least less effective. All graduates must pass a specialty school, in this case Nuclear Power, to continue on in that track in the Navy. I know of no evidence suggesting that English majors are less successful in this than are technical majors, and in any case, they take a math refresher course the summer after they graduate from the Academy.

People ideologically allied with former Secretary of the Navy John Lehman insist that there should be no cap on the percentage of nontechnical majors. Lehman removed the 20-percent cap that had been in effect until then. The argument for not limiting the number of nontechnical majors is that the skills in thinking, communication, and interaction we help foster will be of benefit to the Navy and Marine Corps. The core curriculum and the specialty schools can be counted on to do the rest. This school of thought continues to hold the upper hand, in that there is no formal cap on the number of nontechnical majors. Yet since the removal of the cap, the percentage of nontechnical majors has drifted past 30 percent. The powers-that-be became anxious; currently they reserve the right to assign students to majors if that should be necessary "in the best interests of the Navy," and they try to influence hearts and minds by exhortation: this is a technical institution, students are told.

In the same way that humanities subjects are only one dish in a larger academic meal even for those students who major in them, academics as a whole cumulatively play what I must wryly admit is only a subsidiary role in the larger makeup of Annapolis. Most of our students don't come to the Academy for the classroom experience; more than a few regard it as an onerous blockage between themselves and their commission in the fleet. Our students are constantly preoccupied with things they have to turn in to their "upperclass" or to their company officers, trying to cram in enough homework to "keep their grades up," and complaining about the newest "regs" (regulations) in Bancroft Hall. They are happy if I let them out five minutes early, and happier still on those rare occasions when class is canceled.

The "don't slow me down, sir" attitude of midshipmen that I find more and more bemusing would, I think, seem strange at Annapolis's other institution of higher education, the other place tourists go. Verdant St. John's College is next door to the Academy and yet in some ways light-years away. St. John's is the third-oldest college in the United States, dating back to a precursor institution founded in 1696 (King William's School, as the sign in front of the college tells us). It follows a rigorous curriculum of Great Books beginning with Plato and the pre-Socratics in freshman year and extending to writers as close to contemporary as T.S. Eliot ("Death by Water") and James Joyce in senior year. Science is taught by re-creating the experiments of, say, Archimedes; all the students learn to pick their way through classical Greek. Interestingly enough, this was a curricular change dating from the 1930s; before that, St. John's College was a military school.

St. John's is tucked up against College Creek, down to which its green hill rolls, a piece of prime real estate adjoined by the office buildings for the state government and by eighteenth-century homes along tree-lined brick walkways. The bricks are usually tilted crazily because of the tree roots that refuse to be kept down. St. John's main building, MacDowell Hall—one of the cupolas visible to tourists from the "Scenic Lookout"—was formerly the residence of a Colonial Maryland governor, and it occupies the center of the campus, which opens toward town with an air of receiving its people. A few years ago, the college's august "Liberty Tree," dating from the Revolution and the site of meetings of patriots of the time, finally succumbed to the gradual weakening of time and the sudden blow of lightning. Other trees have been planted in its place, but somehow the campus still looks a bit naked, at least to eyes that remember the Liberty Tree.

The contrast between the two institutions that call Maryland's leafy capital city home could hardly be more stark, though they meet on King George's Street in the heart of Annapolis. In this city, home (as the tour guides tell you) of the State House in longest continuous use in the United States, Athens rubs shoulders with Sparta. Yet the two institutions interact with the social formulae of frigid politeness, like people in an elevator waiting out the ride in uneasy silence. The line of their jointure is along the parking lots of one and the backsides of officer housing for the other, and they are separated by a busy street. They seem coziest where they both run out: their crew boathouses face each other from opposite sides of a bridge on College Creek, far from the ceremonial center of each college.

There have been times when the two institutions have actively clashed. In the waning years of World War II, the Naval Academy attempted what we would now call a hostile takeover of St. John's on the grounds that the Navy, and the nation, needed the buildings and the land to train officers. St. John's narrowly escaped with its life, with one defender noting somewhat acerbically that the purpose of St. John's was to teach people how to avoid having wars. And during the height of the Vietnam War, when short-haired midshipmen were immediately distinguishable from the long-haired "Johnnies" both in appearance and politics, the Johnnies taunted midshipmen by calling them "baby-killers." The mids returned the compliment by saying the Johnnies were Commies and worse. Even now, in an era of universally short collegiate haircuts, you'd have to be unobservant to mistake a Johnnie for a mid on the brick-lined streets of Annapolis.

Of the two institutions, it's the Naval Academy that clearly has the town's heart. The largest single employer in town, the Academy dwarfs St. John's in its physical plant and in the size of its student body. Besides, Annapolis is a nautical town, at the center of Chesapeake Bay. A sign in its Eastport district, across Spa Creek—a sign that briefly stood at the entrance to Annapolis from the highway leading to Washington, D.C.—identifies it as "America's Sailing Capital." Certainly it has as good a claim to that title as, say, Newport.

More to the point perhaps, it's a Navy town. Military retirees have bought up many of the eighteenth- and nineteenth-century townhouses along Annapolis's historic streets, and they use the Academy as their one-stop social club. There's the huge

Annapolis chapter of the Alumni Association, the organization that owns the elegant eighteenth-century brick house across from St. John's; there's the Officers' and Faculty Club (which most retirees insist on calling merely the O Club; as an F, I eke out a feeble revenge by referring to it merely as the F Club); and there are the events open to the public at the Naval Academy: every Friday and Saturday there are, for starters, sports matches.

St. John's doesn't even come close on the popular-appeal meter. The Academy, after all, begs for boosters: it encourages all of Annapolis to come "support the midshipmen" in their games and matches. St. John's, by contrast, being so small and so relentlessly cerebral, doesn't even have most of the usual teams. Compared to the Peloponnesian War, what would a mere game matter? They probably wouldn't even care if they won or not.

There's a lot of local interaction with the Academy. Civilian families sign on to "sponsor" midshipmen, which in practice means to open their houses and refrigerators for the students to use as homes away from home. Midshipmen return the compliment by tutoring in the local schools and picking up trash on Saturday mornings.

Part of the reason Annapolis loves the Academy and merely accepts St. John's is that Johnnies are considerably less picturesque in their daily activities than are the midshipmen. At the Academy there are noon-meal formation and Wednesday parades. Go over to the St. John's campus and, even if the day is nice, you're likely to see nothing more than a few young men and women lying under trees with their brows furrowed by Sophocles. If you're really lucky, they may be playing Frisbee. More likely, they'll be hunched over their texts in seminars or tutorials, or on their tenth cup of coffee in the basement of MacDowell Hall. So, after a glance at the buildings, Victorian additions to the original eighteenth-century house with its newly remodeled library, formerly the Maryland State Hall of Records, the tourists move on to the Naval Academy.

Two Missions

ALTHOUGH SPOKESPEOPLE FOR St. John's note that its graduates go on to be successful in many fields—they can even go to medical school after taking "proper" science courses elsewhere—the college offers an education that is proudly and perhaps somewhat anachronistically liberal, at least in the technical sense of "liberating" and "across disciplines." In the words of its Web site and catalogue.

> St. John's College is a community dedicated to liberal education. Such education seeks to free men and women from the tyrannies of unexamined opinions and inherited prejudices. It also endeavors to enable them to make intelligent, free choices concerning the ends and means of both public and private life.

The Naval Academy is equally sure of its educational goals, which do not include seeking to free men and women from the tyrannies of unexamined opinions and inherited prejudices. Of course, most people would say that the purpose of the education at the Naval Academy, in a narrow sense, is to produce officers in the U.S. Navy and Marine Corps. Not all officers in the Navy and Marine Corps come from Annapolis, but all Annapolis graduates—except for the ten or twelve "international" students given an education as a favor to small client states—do become naval officers. A small handful who can show special justification—usually family histories in the Army or Air Force—can graduate from the Naval Academy and be commissioned into these services. All who graduate serve (except those kicked out for exceptional reasons, usually medical). It's their obligation to pay back the taxpayer-supported education whose monetary value the higher-ups currently like to place upward of $250,000.

This figure seems high, and I wonder where it comes from. Does it include a prorated percentage of building and grounds upkeep? The cost of maintaining the fleet of Navy training boats on the Severn River, the Yard Patrol (YP) boats on which students practice going to sea? The cost of their going on summer cruises on submarines and carriers? It's so huge I suspect it must. However the sum is figured, the fact remains that students are fed, clothed, housed, educated, and trained to use the high-technology weapons of the U.S. Navy for four years: the cost comes out of taxpayers' pockets. They might, I sometimes think, like to know what the purpose and effect of this investment are.

The time of service is most typically five years after the students receive their diplomas, down from six when I arrived. In the case of those who are chosen to become pilots (it's one of the "sexy" alternatives: the movie *Top Gun* is apparently still required viewing for anyone remotely interested in attending Annapolis), the payback is "seven years past wings," the acquisition of their flying certification. It's a training process that itself takes several years, so that the pilots can well end up in their early thirties before they can leave the Navy to fly commercial planes, as many of them end up doing. Or used to. In this era of widespread airline bankruptcy, not even this seems a safe alternative.

Beyond this narrow goal of producing officers in the Navy and Marine Corps, the Naval Academy has a mission statement like—and at the same time completely unlike—St. John's. Midshipmen must learn it by heart, as one of the many things they memorize. It's in the catalogue, on our Web site, and molded in metal on a plaque outside the administration building. Its placement is next to a mast where the Marine Guards from across the river hoist the flag each morning at 0800 and haul it down each day at 1700.

The somewhat long-winded mission of the Academy, according to this plaque by the flagpole where colors are hoisted and lowered, is

> to develop midshipmen morally, mentally and physically and to imbue them with the highest ideals of duty, honor and loyalty in order to provide graduates who are dedicated to a career of naval service and have potential for future development in mind and character to assume the highest responsibilities of command, citizenship and government.

The missions from both Athens and Sparta end up talking about fitting into a larger whole: "public life" at St. John's; "government" at the Naval Academy. But they are different in almost all other respects. For the Naval Academy, students will be developed to some unspecified point "morally, mentally, and physically." Presumably we know what this point is. They can be "imbued with ideals"—again, presumably ideals we can define, goals we can help set for them. In the view of the Naval Academy, therefore, education moves a student outward to some external goal. According to St. John's, by contrast, education is in a sense negative: it removes impediments, frees men and women from the tyranny of received opinions. Nor is there any mention in the St. John's mission statement of knowing what it is we want the individual to become. Each person will become something different.

Caught by Colors

THE FLAGPOLE NEXT to the Academy's mission statement plays a large role in determining the rhythm of our day. A bugler plays either "Reveille" or "Taps," depending on which end of the day it is. While this is taking place, midshipmen, officers, and faculty are frozen in their tracks, brought to attention by the sound of the bugle and now standing rigid and immobile along walkways, facing (even if through the visually impenetrable side of a building) the place where the flag is known to be, like a Muslim praying toward Mecca, however far away it is, the military saluting until the bugler gives the flourish that signals "all clear." Suddenly the spell is lifted, like Snow White being kissed by her prince, and they move on to their destinations.

Back when, as a newly arrived faculty member, I had to teach classes that started at 0755, and I would occasionally get students arriving ten minutes late, huffing and puffing: "I got caught by colors, sir," they say. They had been on a walkway, running to class already late, and were enchanted by the spell of the bugle, unable to move until liberated by the same sorcerer.

It's bad for them when they're late. The computer module on which I must daily report absences and latenesses to my classes gives me the option, under "Tardy" (other options include "Left Early" or "Absent"), calibrated with great precision, each increment making that much more reprehensible the infraction: 1 MINUTE, 2 MINUTES, 3 MINUTES, 4 MINUTES, 5 MINUTES—then it jumps to 10 MINUTES and 15 MINUTES. If I enter any of these, or "Absent," the student him- or herself already has to have signed the log book back in the Hall to indicate that s/he was late or absent, and give the reason why. Lack of a sanctioned justification produces a punishment. Needless to say, oversleeping and "I didn't feel like going to class" do not count as justifications. At Annapolis, class attendance is a military obligation. Why not? The taxpayers are paying us to teach, and paying for the students to come to class. Of course, what they take "on board" (as we say) from their time in the classroom is another story.

Entries in this log book are made all in capital letters, written out by hand, sometimes at great speed. It's a style of writing that I find my own hand incapable of producing, and that I know only as one font possibility on the computer. Frequently the students carry this means of writing over to the notes they sometimes tack on my door: SIR, I CAME BY TO SEE IF YOU WERE HERE AND MISSED YOU. VERY RESPECT-FULLY, MIDN 4/C SMITH. I feel that I am being shouted at, or talked to by a robot. Sometimes their officers, unaware of how odd this looks to a civilian, will send "all-hands" e-mails that scream off the screen in the same way; these I can simply delete. Then again, maybe they do know it looks like shouting. Shouting is the norm at Annapolis: that's useful for me, because I find I can sometimes get their attention by whispering.

When I first arrived at the Academy, absences were noted not by the professor but by the student "section leader," in what was surely an attempt to transfer some initiative to the students. I was supposed to pick the two midshipmen with the highest and second-highest ranks in the brigade for a section leader and assistant section leader. I never did. Stripes (metal bars joined together in a parallel block on the collar) denote responsibility; seniors can have anywhere from none ("Midshipman in ranks") to six stripes (the Brigade Commander), so giving one of these positions to someone who already had a time-consuming job in the hall would pile more onto his or her already over-full plate. I chose the leader and assistant on whims. Beginnings or endings of the alphabet seemed a bit obvious as principles of choice, so I chose the two people in the middle of the alphabet, or the tallest and the shortest, or two women (to make a point), or two students who, in the first few minutes of the first class, struck me as people who might reasonably be assumed to have a bit more on the ball than the others.

The section leader was also supposed to give the "attention on deck," at which the students spring to attention as I enter the classroom, and to "give the muster" at the beginning of class: either "All present or accounted for, sir," or the list of who wasn't there, while the students stood stiffly next to their desks. At some point the administration discovered that somehow no one was ever absent, and they took back this responsibility from the students. Now, if I have failed to report absences by two days after a class, I get an admonishing if electronically-produced e-mail asking me to do so.

When the section leader was in charge of this, my responsibility ended with entering his or her name and "alpha" into the computer—the "alpha" being the Academy equivalent of a Social Security number: a six-digit number that is an absolute identifier of the person, always beginning with the last two digits of his or her year of graduation. I remember, at new-faculty orientation when I arrived, that the Navy captain who spoke to us told us proudly of a venerable faculty member who was able to remember the alpha of all his students. When he'd pass them on the walk, he'd address them by this number, as in: "Good Morning, 584331!" Orwellian echoes aside, I could never figure out if this man thought the students liked this or was simply showing off his prodigious memory for numbers—nor whether the captain admired him or found him bizarre.

Once I had entered their alphas, it was their military obligation to put in the absences. Back in the Stone Age of computer use by institutions, about the time I was coming to the Academy, all programs for some reason ended in ***, pronounced "triple star." If the person the computer knew to be the section leader failed to enter absences, he or she was immediately hunted down by a program called DEFIANT***, pronounced "Defiant Triple-Star." For many years, Defiant Triple-Star seemed to me the military's ultimate malediction.

The command "attention on deck" is, of course, adopted

from the Navy proper. It provides only one example of the metaphor we live daily at the Academy: we are a ship. Working this metaphor to exhaustion produces a large proportion of the jargon for our jargon-heavy existence. Students ask to use the "head" (a toilet, called "the head" not in an anatomical reference but because at one point it was a place off the bow, or head, of the ship where sailors relieved themselves directly into the deep). My office is on the "second deck" of Sampson Hall. A "p-way" (passageway) rather than a hallway joins the offices. Students don't sleep, they "rack out" on their "racks" (beds). Sometimes whimsical poetry takes over from the nautical terminology: the "issue" (standard issue) blue blankets on midshipmen racks is called their "Blue Magnet," because it draws them into its embrace.

Into Battle

ATHENS AND SPARTA do interact. The two schools meet for battle, as the Navy sees it, every spring in the annual USNA–St. John's croquet game, which is always held at St. John's. It's virtually the only organized contact between St. John's and the Naval Academy, and it has become an Annapolis social event. People from town bring picnic baskets and loll over the verdant lawns in front of MacDowell Hall, dressed in their Gatsbyesque best: vests and white flannel pants for men and gauzy summer wear complete with garden-party floppy hats for women. Indeed, one of the more striking aspects of this event is its sartorial splendor, duly noted a few years back in an article in *GQ* magazine. The midshipmen, all from the same company year after year, used to pair the white pants and shoes from their summer uniforms with the tops of their SDBs, and add the bow ties from their "mess dress"—yet another uniform, with a waiter's fitted jacket and a gold cummerbund and tie—to create something like summer-stock 1920s garb. Recently they've gone upscale, with white sports sweaters and ties over their white pants.

The Johnnies on the croquet team stand out because of their lack of this nattiness, wearing their usual blue jeans, or thrift-shop chic, or sometimes camouflage complete with face paint. For Johnnie supporters, the sky's the limit: one woman at a recent match wore flowing "Grecian" chiffon and a pair of huge gossamer wings, perhaps in homage to the Louvre's *Winged Victory*—though her arms, in contrast to those of the statue, were intact, sporting fetching "Grecian" circlets above her elbows.

It's usual for the Johnnies to win this battle. As the mids point out scoffingly, they practice this stuff over at St. John's. From the midshipmen point of view, it's only croquet. At least, this used to be the attitude; now I hear the midshipmen are getting more cutthroat. It's their competitive spirit rising to the challenge. Still, they typically like sports that involve a bit more muscle and blood, like football or boxing. Brigade boxing finals draws a roaring crowd into the Field House, and everyone must take the sport as part of physical education—even women, who box other women.

Beat Army, Sir!

YET THE INSTITUTION with which the Naval Academy compares itself most often is not its geographical neighbor, so different from it in so many ways. It is, of course, the Military Academy, West Point, home of the "Black Knights"—"Army" as we are "Navy." Army is forty-one years older than Navy, perhaps because it took the new nation longer to scrape the money together to build boats than it did to field an army. Army is our nemesis. It is the Enemy.

At each "squared corner" in Bancroft Hall, newly arrived plebes must yell something: "Beat Army Sir!" is one of the more popular choices. The national anthem at Navy events always ends with a hearty cheer of "Beat Army!" as does the alma mater, "Navy Blue and Gold." All the forty-five-pound plates in the weight rooms say "Beat Army" in letters embossed in the metal, painted gold for contrast against the blue background. As the signs on the walls tell you, "Beat Army" has to be facing out when you put the plates on the bar.

In the varsity-athletes' weight room, a metal plaque tells us that the facility is dedicated to those graduates "who gave their lives in service to their country." "May their souls rest in peace," it continues, and then comes its benediction: "Go Navy. Beat Army." The first time I saw this I smiled and simultaneously blinked back tears, reading it by myself in the Valhalla of this so-perfect weight room, where the fifty-five-pound dumbbell is where a label says the fifty-five-pound dumbbell will be, and where the bench-press bars are actually stripped of metal discs after use, as they are supposed to be—and rarely are—in other weight rooms. I am charmed by the thought of the Army-Navy rivalry extending even to heaven.

Our rivalry with Army is absolute, the two institutions providing the Manichaean poles of our existence: Navy Good, Army Bad. It's something of a reality check to realize that all this in fact centers on nothing more than an annual football contest. A recent book by John Feinstein called *A Civil War: Army vs. Navy* charts what the author calls "college football's purest rivalry." Certainly the annual December game provides the grand finale for the fall semester, and, by extension, for much of the rest of the year. When we "Beat Army, sir!" it seems that our team not only beats their team; our Academy beats their Academy, our uniformed service beats their uniformed service. We show our disdain, and our supremacy, by successfully kidnapping their mascot, a mule, while simultaneously trying to ensure that they do not kidnap our mascot, a goat. Well, not any goat. Bill the Goat, whom I rely on increasingly to teach plebe writers that they must think of their audience. "Tell Bill," I say, it seems like a thousand times a semester. He has to be useful for more than decorating spirit buttons.

The Army-Navy game typically takes place a week before the end of classes. I know by now I'll get no work out of the students the week before, and none the week after either, in what is clearly a lame-duck time in the semester. The week before, the students stay up at night playing what they think of as jokes on one another and the higher-ups. They arrive in class with their faces glowing and then hurry to tell me about their exploits: they have filled their company officer's room with wadded-up newspaper; they have "pennied-in" a fellow midshipman's room, gleefully explaining that putting a row of pennies in the minuscule crack between a dorm-room door and the frame makes opening it impossible.

As the week goes on, they become even more than usually sleep-deprived. It's like watching the liquid slowly drain out of the glass as their energy ebbs. They sleep on the busses up to the game, they tell me. And then it's game time, and they explode.

Thinking 101

THE FRESHMAN ENGLISH course that all members of our department teach as part of their load, no matter how senior they are, should—I sometimes muse—be called "Thinking 101." My students, like college freshmen almost everywhere, understand neither how to make an argument nor how to get beyond the self-evidence of their own beliefs. Each year, my struggle is to convince them that most of life does not fall into the extremes of black and white, but is, as most adults know, firmly mired in the spectrum of grays. Since all of their other classes and the rest of their life at the Academy take place in the comforting realm of absolutes, they are puzzled. For them, this shows only the uselessness of such "soft" subjects as English. Again and again I must convince them that written objects, such as stories or poems, merit a reader's careful attention: it is not good enough for them to take a flying leap over a text, attach to it some personal associations that have nothing to do with anyone else's (their most frequent thoughts are what it "reminds them of"), and then pitch the book back onto the shelf in order to go on to the next task in a day already over-filled with tasks.

On the days when I feel sorry for myself, it all seems particularly thankless. To start with, there's the relentlessly anti-intellectual cast of the institution itself: being good in school isn't cool. The Hall, Bancroft Hall, fills their time with so much relentless trivia that they never have a chance simply to sit and let the pieces digest. Then there's the gender angle, especially sharp at this male-run and -dominated school. Men exhibit their masculinity by grunting at each other and out-bench-pressing the next guy, not by spinning reams of perfect prose. English is sissy.

A perhaps closet-Marxist colleague suggested to me last year another interpretation of our school's ethos, an economic one. Our students are so impervious to our intervention because they don't think of themselves as paying money for what we do. Their payback, in the form of military service, comes after graduation, and so is too far away to compute in their still-adolescent minds. You only appreciate what you put money in the box for: if the price tag is evident, you begin to value it, make it part of your calculations. So instead of demanding that they get value for money, they ask only that no demands at all be made on them; effectively, that they be cheated.

Then there's the Freudian interpretation that is more congenial to me. Having all their subjects forced down their throat makes them—I realized wearily after many years—passive-aggressive. They have to come to class, but we can't make them like it. So I have to win by force and sheer energy. I fire questions at them, needle them, make them stand up and jump around to wake up, and perhaps, if I'm lucky, get them interested in literature—because I refuse to go away, and getting interested is the easiest way to get past me.

It's fun taking on a new classroom of plebes: not all the learning in the world would protect me from them. Winning them over each time, which usually takes a couple of weeks and in difficult cases as many as six or eight, feels like a small, but real, victory over the world, and an honest one, not achieved by fakery. It's as if, before a fight, I make a pile of my clothing, my degrees, my expensive watch, and anything else that identifies me as being of a higher rank, and then try to win by sheer skill. Each time it happens, I have once again earned the right to say: I've still got what it takes. But should I have to do this? And should it be a fight at all?

What's still hard for me is knowing that to them, I'm not one of the liberators; I'm one of the jailors. They're grinding out work to keep me satisfied, putting in time with me, as they are in the rest of their lives here at USNA, waiting for it to wash over their heads, eternally counting down to the next immediate goal. What a far cry from the way I regarded my own professors at Haverford College, as guides who could show me how to find myself. Our students aren't trying to find themselves. Many of them don't even know there's a self to find, or they assume the search is a trivial thing, long since accomplished. The years will surprise them, I think.

For years, we in the English department have been fielding what I take to be justified complaints by flag officers that our graduates can't express themselves in written form. I once listened to the Academy-graduate skipper of an Aegis cruiser, on which a handful of us civilian English professors were guests, talk for fully twenty minutes about how inept his junior officers were at writing. He spent half his time, he told us, correcting the grammar on the memos that came across his desk. In his parting words, he begged us to go back and give the midshipmen hell. I sure try.

I say to students until I'm weary, "Justify your assertion." "Write for Bill"—the Goat. Bill needs to know things like (surprise!) what book they're writing about, who it's by, and that (say) "Paul," to whom they refer in the first paragraph is (gosh!) the book's protagonist. Bill also needs to be able to understand the essay-writer's point very early on, and to be led with as few missteps as possible through an argument that actually defends the points the writer says he or she is going to defend. Bill gets very angry when writers don't satisfy his need for things like commas to make sentences comprehensible, when they betray lack of knowledge of a difference between plural and possessive, and when they fail to use words in the same way that others use them, rather than as they think, in some alternative universe, such words could and should be used. I'm not sure our plebes ever understand about having to justify their views rather than merely asserting them ever more loudly—too often the recourse of politicians, and of the military. They think I'm full of hot air when I talk about the gray area we all navigate in, the way we use objectivity to buttress subjectivity. Everything has to have a simple answer; they just haven't found it yet. If I were a nice guy, I'd just give them the "gouge"—the bottom line, the right answer— and be done with it.

Civilian vs. Military

OFFICIALLY, THE NAVAL Academy insists that there is a fifty-fifty military/civilian split among faculty members. This may be close to technically true, but I think it probably counts the company officers as well as all the temporary "stash" ensigns putting in a few months before going on to specialty school. Certainly it isn't true for most of the core academic subjects. I've come to believe that the vaunted fifty-fifty split is an article of faith rather than a figure arrived at empirically, something that betokens a comfortable level of integration we may not, in fact, have achieved. The cast of the institution as a whole is military, yet civilians are the majority in our academic departments, overwhelmingly so in the case of such departments as English and History.

Annapolis is the only one of the academies that began life

with a mixture of civilian and military faculty members. In the last few years, the other academies have acquired a few civilians too. I suspect this is largely because, in this era of military parsimony, civilian professors like me who arrive at the door with a Ph.D. in hand come cheaper than military faculty, whose bills are paid by Uncle Sam. It hasn't always been a comfortable mix at Annapolis. There were periods in the nineteenth century, I have read, when civilians were all but eliminated from the teaching staff as a result of the suspicion that they were gumming up the works. Now in the era of tenure, we can't be eliminated. But during stormy periods, we can be lectured at.

Unsurprisingly, most of our Naval-Officer faculty members are in departments like Naval Architecture, Seamanship and Navigation, or Professional Development. In English, we have to scrounge, partly because the Navy is notoriously unsupportive of educating its officers, especially in English. There have been periods where we have had more Air Force than Navy officers in the department.

Most of the Naval uniforms we see in our department carry the collar insignia or shoulder boards of lieutenants, and are worn by men and a few women who are typically twenty-eight to thirty years old, English majors—usually from right here at the Academy—who have been off for five years flying airplanes or driving ships (as they say), and who have been approved for one reason or another to come back to teach. Many of them lack any professional credentials beyond the Academy's B.S. (All students here get a Bachelor of Science degree, even if their degree is in English or one of the other nontechnical disciplines.) In one classroom of plebes, therefore, the adult at the front of the room may be a full professor with decades of experience. In the one next door, he or she may be a newly returned aviator whose own education stopped with a bachelor's degree.

These returning lieutenants are expected, to be sure, to be working on a master's degree. In recent years, many of them have done so at St. John's, amusingly enough, and apparently they enjoy the experience. The St. John's master's degree is in Liberal Studies, a short form of the undergraduate curriculum, full of big ideas. I can't say it's not useful in teaching our plebes. The question is moot, since usually the awarding of the degree precedes "rotation" by only a few months, or even weeks—"rotation" out to another job with the fleet, that is, away from the "shore tour" they have just completed.

I sometimes wonder why the institution needs people with PhDs, if lieutenants with bachelor's degrees are fine too. Not that I think degrees matter a darn with our students. I have to use much more elemental means to reach them than mere book-learning.

Maybe it's better that way. In my first year, I asked them to call me Mr. Fleming. That, after all, is what we called professors at Haverford and Bryn Mawr, because of *course* they all had PhDs.; it wasn't cool to insist on the obvious. I soon realized this was misplaced modesty: they themselves were Mr. and Miss, and they had no clue I might actually have a professional credential. It seemed tacky to ask to be called "Doctor" (the sign of a small-town institution like Salisbury State College, now Salisbury University, where my parents taught). And "Professor," my actual rank in the Navy system (even an assistant professor is addressed as "Professor," the way a lieutenant commander can be addressed as "Commander") sounded too much like something out of a Chautauqua from 1872: "Strike up the band, Professor!" Still, of the choices, it seemed the most justifiable.

At Annapolis, degrees may be meaningless, but it's not in the same way they are at Haverford. Our students don't challenge the person in front of them, the way I remember doing in college: Who *are* you? What justifies your taking my time? What is your specialty? What are your books? Instead, they're resigned: I've been assigned to them, and they to me. Their schedule says "Professor Fleming," so Professor Fleming it is.

Just before my arrival at the Academy in 1987, we apparently went through a turbulent period in which military seemed aligned against civilian, at least in the English department. (The current commandant of the Marine Corps was our division director early in my years at the Academy, and an excellent one who is still remembered fondly. His point of departure was clearly that we knew what we were doing unless we proved otherwise. I recommend this as an effective way of dealing with adults.) The division director at the time had rooted out what he apparently thought was a bed of civilian sedition. Among other things, I hear, one of the faculty members was teaching a now largely forgotten essay called "Madeline Among the Midshipmen," written by an officer named William Edward Wilson and assigned to the English department at Annapolis during the 1940s.

This diverting essay recounts the author's amusement at teaching midshipmen Keats's narrative poem "The Eve of St.

Agnes," whose heroine is the essayist's eponymous Madeline. The author gets a good chuckle, which he shares with the reader, out of the fact that one midshipman, presenting in class the stanza in which Keats tells us that "out went the taper" (the candle went out), spoke knowledgeably of the "large animal" rushing from the room. He had undoubtedly imagined a "tapir," which he apparently thought an unsurprising resident of Medieval castle bedrooms.

Wilson subsequently recounts that when the class had turned to Percy Bysshe Shelley's "Hymn to Intellectual Beauty," a senior officer lectured Wilson on the deleterious effects on the midshipmen's manhood of teaching the works of a poet named Percy. This was the more to be feared as this particular Percy was someone who, by his own admission, had—or at least his narrative persona had—"clasp'd his hands and shrieked." Clasping hands wasn't manly, and shrieking even less so. Yelling in battle was, of course, fine.

This essay seemed to the then–division director to be critical of the Naval Academy and all it stood for, and teaching it disrespectful, outrageous behavior on the part of these unruly civilians. He instituted a military department chair to tighten things up, and he was looking into the war credentials of those who were hired. I'm told I got in only because this chairman, who turned out to be a complete sweetheart rather than the anticivilian martinet the director, by then gone, had evidently hoped for, assured him I'd been too young for Vietnam. This particular division director was a man whose name is synonymous with Vietnam-era bravery, and whose exploits are in fact memorialized in a tiny lit-up diorama in Memorial Hall that looks like a killing-fields version of the tiny doll rooms in Chicago's Field Museum and the Baltimore Museum of Art.

It wasn't quite true that I'd been too young for Vietnam. A wannabe hippie in my small-town high school, where protesting against the war meant you were someone interesting, I was entered for the draft lottery the year I turned eighteen, in 1972. My number, somewhere in the 90s as I recall, was sufficient to keep me out; they only called into the 40s. The peace talks were shortly to begin, and the war was winding down. And that was that.

It may be that the reason I find our interactions with the Navy so bemusing is that there is no "how-to" course for civilian professors. We pass a background check, sign a statement saying we understand our obligations, and, after a rather general two-day orientation, are simply thrown in the water to swim. We dress in suits and ties rather than uniforms, are supposed to wear our official ID cards "visible and above the waist" (few of us do), teach our classes, and fulfill our administrative functions. The pretense of the institution is that there is nothing peculiar that we have to learn; we do our job, end of story.

When asked what it's like to teach at Annapolis, only two extreme kinds of answer are possible. Of course, there's the long version, as I'm giving here, with all the nuances and ramifications: that midshipmen are, in a complex way, different. Yet the easier, shorter version, the one I give at cocktail parties, is that midshipmen are like students everywhere except that they wear uniforms. "They're nice kids," I always add.

"And disciplined too!" my interlocutor typically cues me.

"Sure," I say, refusing to engage further. If I bit on that, I'd be on the slippery slope to the long version: disciplined, but at a price; disciplined, but on the surface; disciplined, but only in body, not in mind. The surface differences between academic life for me here and a comparable life elsewhere are so evident that we agree to overlook them, in best "Purloined Letter" style. And the fundamental differences are pieced together out of a thousand examples that take a while to give.

The differences between midshipmen and other students, aside from the too-obvious-to-bear-comment fact of their uniforms, are below the surface, and they do require the long version for me even to get near expressing them. To someone shadowing me for A Day in the Life of a Civilian Professor, my life would seem essentially identical to one I'd lead at another college. We neither salute nor are saluted, cannot use the PX (Post Exchange) on the other side of the river (only recently have we had access to the bookstore on a regular basis), are not covered by military insurance or retirement, and have our own pay system. As it happens, this isn't particularly generous. Many years ago, USNA faculty members were well compensated compared to their counterparts at civilian colleges; this advantage was eroded and disappeared long ago. The rewards of teaching here, as perhaps of the military in general, are of other sorts.

Things that are mandatory for the military aren't so for us. We don't suffer inspection on the days new uniforms come in, and the person who writes our "fitrep," our fitness report, is the civilian chair of the department, not the senior officer. The differences between my life at Annapolis and the life I'd lead at another institution appear like the tremors of earthquakes, unpredictable until you figure out where the tectonic plates are. It takes a while.

Bull Major

WHEN I ARRIVED at the Naval Academy, English was still referred to as a "bull" major, as in, of course, bullshit. To be sure, some attempt was made on occasion to deny this clear origin by citing a physically prepossessing professor in the early years of the century known as "Bull," the way Admiral Halsey of World War II fame was known as "Bull." No one believed this. This term "bull major" was not only part of the rich trove of Naval Academy slang, but a required vocabulary term on the list of insider jargon that students memorized from *Reef Points* during plebe summer.

I protested this fact in a letter to the superintendent. It was a time of other vocabulary changes as well: along about the same time, terms derogatory to women (such as "WUBA," an official acronym for a female midshipman, usually held by the male midshipmen to mean "Women Used By All") were also being removed from *Reef Points*. The Superintendent had to concur that the term "bull major" was, in fact, derogatory, and it too was duly removed from its officially sanctioned spot.

I adhere to the sentiment expressed by a T-shirt I sometimes see in the weight room: the universal sign for negation, a circle with a diagonal cross-out bar, over the single word "whining." But why should I put up with teaching something the institution I teach in branded officially as hot air, or excrement? To me that would have been accepting official second-class citizenship. Still, the old guard is probably smiling at the fact that the term "bull major" has survived in *Reef Points* despite me, buried in the definition of another of the terms whose assimilation continues to be required, "happiness factor." Somehow the idea is that you're happier if you've taken a "bull major," though of course personal happiness, far from being the goal, is rather suspect. If you're having a good time, something has to be wrong.

The Naval Academy is an institution with a long tradition of happily offensive terminology, so it could be argued that this was all good clean fun. When my ex–father-in-law went here in the 1940s, graduating early to take part in World War II, the foreign language he took was "dago." Indeed, all foreign languages were "dagos." His particular dago was Portuguese, though others took German or French as their dago.

Though my institution doesn't any more, at least not too overtly, brand what I do as "bull," it still manages to make clear that it remains suspicious of what those people over in the English department are up to. The pieces I publish periodically on the Naval Academy sometimes meet with hostile reactions like those inspired by the teaching of "Madeline Among the Midshipmen." These tend not to come from the higher-ups, who in all but one more recent case acknowledge in public my right to a professional judgment, whatever they may say in private. Typically, the most outraged responses come from mid-level officers teaching in the "Professional Development" or "Leadership" departments, who clearly consider themselves guardians of public morality.

A few years ago, I ended one such piece with the line, "What have we done?" The day after it appeared in the *Chronicle of Higher Education,* I received an irate e-mail from an officer ranting about the incalculable harm I had caused the Academy through the less-than-completely-positive view I had presented in public. His invective ended with what he clearly intended to be a biting indictment: "What have *you* done?"

On my bad days, or bad weeks, I worry that what my Marine plebe pointed out is true: what we are teaching isn't very motivational. But then I am strong. We're not educating "grunts," but future officers. And future officers have to deal with a lot of situations that aren't "motivational." Talking with flag officers convinces me that being an officer isn't about easy yes/no decisions. It's about maturity, about realizing that people are unpredictable, and about being able to think on your feet. And that's what we say we in the English department are there for. We like to say that we help two-thirds of the mission, the mental and moral parts. Can military and civilian education be combined? Or do they merely coexist?

Essays

FREQUENTLY, I ASK the midshipmen to write their first essays on their summer introduction to the Naval Academy, a topic still fresh in their minds. This fall: "The Most Unexpected Aspect of Plebe Summer." Many of them record details that I am now familiar with: the constant pressure from the upperclassmen and -women who are there to "indoctrinate" them (the word is used at the Academy without embarrassment), who scream questions at them, and who demand that they produce laboriously memorized lists of names and the day's menu; the inch-by-inch inspection of their rooms and persons for dust or uncleanliness; the early-morning physical exercises that few of them are prepared for.

Two essays one year were particularly touching. For one student, the most unexpected aspect of plebe summer was its emphasis on teamwork. An only child, the student wrote that he had always done everything alone. His first day at the Academy, he set his alarm clock so that he would be early for formation. He writes how he arrived without his roommates. "Where are your classmates?" the upperclassman screamed. "Do you think you are better than they are?" "Sir, no, sir . . ." the plebe began, but then he was on the ground, doing push-ups until his classmates arrived. (Now punishment push-ups, as in the bellowed "DROP AND GIVE ME TWENTY!," have been banned.) The point, he spelled out, still in wonder, is: at this institution you never do anything alone.

I sat over this paper for longer than usual, rereading the student's carefully memorized rationalization for this rule: that in battle, all must help the others. I am the way this plebe once was and has now learned not to be. I still, in a metaphorical sense, set my alarm to be early at formation; this is how I have learned to regulate my life. And yet the purpose of the student's paper is to show how wrong this is. Is it a recantation, I wonder, like that in a Stalinist show trial? In any case, it is proof that the system has done its work well.

Of course, the paradox is that the plebes spend inordinate amounts of time finding ways to salvage the few remaining shreds of their individuality. They always end up seeming immature. One woman admitted to keeping a goldfish above the suspended ceiling of her room, the only place beside the laundry bag that escaped inspection, for the express purpose of knowing that she was contravening the regulation forbidding pets. They like the fact that they are getting away with something the System has overlooked, in a touching effort to salvage some illusion of personal control. Their nocturnal journeys over our ineffectual brick Wall are another way they have of keeping some vestige of self-determination. We haven't made them honest; we've just made them devious—and reduced them to ridiculous attempts to salvage something of themselves; attempts whose energy could have been put to the greater good under other circumstances.

The other paper over which I lingered—moving rapidly through those that are just badly organized, or so full of idealistic clichés that I can barely bring myself to read them—was about the Honor Concept. (A student guilty of, say, cheating, is found "in violation of the Honor Concept": what does it mean, I wonder, to be in violation of a concept?) That was, for this student, the most unexpected aspect of the summer.

He had done something wrong, whereupon his roommate was assigned to write a page-long essay in punishment. (A punishment essay!) The student tells how he tried to help his roommate by writing the essay for him. Somehow it came out who had in fact written the essay. Then the ax fell: my plebe, the real author of the punishment essay, was called on the carpet the next day by his upperclassman, who informed him that he had committed an honor violation for which he could be thrown out—separated, to use the Academy euphemism that always makes me think of what happens when the wallpaper paste dries out, a slow process rather than the ripping apart that is closer to reality.

This paper, at any rate, was well written: the student reproduced every tremor, every nuance of his horrified realization that he has made a mistake, the system has found him out; he fears being sent home in disgrace. The suspense goes on until the last page, where the upperclassman tells him that this one time, the violation will go unreported (this is one option in the honor code of the Academy, to "counsel" and not press charges). The paper ended with a rush of reconstructed relief: the student feels only gratitude that he was spared to write about it in English class.

I limited myself, in correcting the paper, to a few observations on content: Could he have developed this? I asked in my scrawl—increasingly illegible, it seems, as the years go by. If he accepts that the system would have been justified in booting him for this action—I ask—how can he accept its letting him stay?

Of course the question was unfair: I am just articulating my own reflections on the essentialist notion of honor that prevails here. Is it even possible to achieve the dream of honor and purity that the Academy represents to most of them, in a prelude to the equally touching dream of glory on the battlefield in which plebes, at any rate, still firmly believe?

At the Army-Navy
Poetry Playoffs

ON THE DAY in 1991 before the ground war was declared in what we now call the First Persian Gulf War, I find myself on my way to West Point, the more immediate Enemy. The six other people in one of two vans that roll through the too brightly lit stage set of the New Jersey Turnpike are midshipmen. We are going to our sister military academy, in this time of war, to read poetry.

Back at Annapolis, since it is the weekend, upperclass midshipmen are out on dates, or wandering about downtown Annapolis in same-sex pairs, clad in their navy-blue coats and identical-issue snow-white scarves; plebes are studying. All of them watch CNN for a few moments when they can, just to get an update on the war—those in town by ducking into bars, those in the Yard somewhat more concertedly in the wardrooms, between bites of Friday-night junk food.

All in all, however, the impending war has affected our lives very little. To be sure, when I enter the classroom and the students jump to attention at the section leader's command of "attention on deck," the television in the front of the room was on, tuned either to the news or to the Naval Academy's internal channel. But we don't talk about war in class. We continue, as before, with *Candide* (free will vs. determinism), with A.E. Housman ("loveliest of trees, the cherry now"), with the exercises in creative writing (imagine a family photograph and recreate the scene leading up to it).

The following day, at West Point, I reflect anew that its buildings have none of the charm of those at Annapolis; the Naval Academy's situation as part of a tourist-friendly eighteenth-century town is quite different from West Point's splendid isolation here among the hills at this curve of the Hudson, where the river speeds up and goes a hundred and thirty feet deep around a narrow outcropping of rock. Almost all the buildings are gray and massive, brazen in their ugliness, as if the architects had simply given up and pretended they'd meant it all to look this way. Most buildings mime battlements and fortresses.

Our meeting of creative-writing students is, however, in a Greek-revival hall that, on our drive-through in the dark the night before, I had decided was the museum. Instead, it turned out to be the equivalent of Memorial Hall at Annapolis, a military necropolis. Upstairs there is a ballroom with portraits of graduates who have made history: Sherman, Grant, Lee, Patton. The walls leading down the stairs are encrusted with tablets to the memory of graduates killed in nineteenth- and early-twentieth-century wars. Those who had the misfortune to die in more recent wars and conflicts, where the casualties were more numerous and the deaths as a result somehow less personal, receive only a mention on a larger tablet, their names smaller.

My West Point counterpart, an Army major and a '72 West Point graduate, point out to a colleague of mine from Annapolis who has come in the other van the radical falling off of deaths in the last years of the Vietnam conflict: West Pointers, he conclude, were not sent in appreciable numbers after about 1970. My colleague nods; I am already on my way downstairs.

We go into a room with wing chairs and Oriental carpets; there are introductions. We take seats, facing—counterintuitively—away from an extraordinary view of the Hudson; the sun is shining on the hills beyond. The announcement is made that the ground war in the Gulf has begun the night before; everyone knows this already, and we go on immediately.

The West Pointers, being the hosts, begin; the leader of their creative-writing club is a young man dressed in camouflage with combat boots. This weekend is also Army-Navy Winter Sports Weekend; wearing cammies, their camouflage uniforms, is a sign of spirit. It is motivational. In fact, our group is not the only group of midshipmen at West Point this weekend. The wrestling matches have taken place just before our gathering— Navy has won, so the midshipmen are pleased. Indeed, some of my students back at Annapolis joked with me a few days before: they asked if I was coach of the Varsity Poetry Reading Team, and as a send-off gave me a hearty "Beat Army!"

This young man—I have not caught his name and must look at his tag when I address him (military name tags are a fabulous invention, I think not for the first time)—begins with a reading from Shelley's *A Defence of Poetry* about the superiority of poetry over things of everyday life. The assembled students are respectfully silent when he is finished, and then someone asks, to indicate both solemnity and appreciation: "What is there to say?" All nod.

I look at my colleague. If he is troubled, he is putting on a brave face. So, for that matter, am I. The young man in combat boots introduces me. At Annapolis, I explain, creative writing is a course like any other in which the students receive grades that become part of their grade-point averages. These averages are important to them not because they help determine admission to a graduate school, as they would at most institutions, but because they determine rank in class, which in turn determines whether the student will be allowed his or her first choice of service selection: nuclear power, surface warfare, submarines. (This was soon to change.)

Even poetry has a practical application at Annapolis, I sometimes think—this one if no other. At West Point, by contrast, I have learned that creative writing is not a course and no credit is given; instead the Poetry Society meets weekly, or biweekly, usually in the absence of a faculty member. How amazing, I think: such dedication. The cadets around me hold dog-eared notebooks in which they have written their poems, some embellished with drawings or pertinent photographs.

The first one to read student-produced work is a female cadet. She is strikingly attractive, despite—or because of—her combat gear. Pale white skin, a hairstyle that conforms to the exigencies of necessary shortness without seeming chopped-off, evident curves beneath her camouflage. I talked with her over coffee only minutes before: her parents are artists, she told me. Professionals, at an art school.

"What are you doing here?" I asked.

"Well," she said, "most artists I know are a little bit flaky. I wanted to do something for the non-flaky side of me for a while—later I may write."

I was entranced, so much so that I nearly missed the hubbub caused by the discovery of a wet teabag an unthinking cadet or midshipman had put on the naked surface of the polished wooden table: we smeared the spot with mayonnaise from a sandwich.

When, a few minutes later, she begins to read, I realize that her poem is bad—something about sitting in a museum. She apologizes to the cadets after the end, acknowledging that they have all heard the poem before. Do these students have their Poetry Club party pieces? I wonder. Do they read the same mediocre poems over and over again?

She tells the story behind her poem's production, "explains" it through an exhaustive catalogue of her intentions. This, I am to find over the next day and a half, is the norm for the cadets. All add the commentary of the story of the poem's production. None asks if this is relevant or irrelevant, already indicated in the text or utterly absent from it. The midshipmen, perhaps as the result of their classes—or of the last-minute coaching session in the van on the way up—are more prepared to be analytical: does line X really contribute to the poem; what is the effect of word Y? I am pleased.

We alternate, Army with Navy. Perhaps the midshipmen back at Annapolis were right: this is taking on the atmosphere of a poetry match after all. One of my students reads a piece I have heavily edited. I want to explain how it is better now than before, and why, but I restrain myself, looking out the window at the sun on the late-winter hills beyond, the swath of the river that is visible from this point on the bluffs. A cadet reads, then a midshipman. I make a few comments, as do others. I am diplomatic, loose: this is all for fun, and it's a weekend.

The cadet who follows speaks with an audible twinge of Georgia or Alabama. Stiff red hair sticks out of the top of his head like a brush. He is obviously uncomfortable, and he prefaces his reading by saying that this is something quite different from what we have heard before. It is an open letter to war protesters, accusing them of being less than honorable Americans, asking why they stab the troops in the back. I sit back and smile inwardly. No contradictions here, no Athens vs. Sparta. This is all Sparta.

The delicate poem of another boy who follows is, by contrast, all Athens. He is a midshipman. I know him; he is the best writer I know at the Academy. His poem is about the throat of a woman seen in a park. His girlfriend (he has told me) is a Quaker; he understands by talking with her that not everyone wants to be defended, certainly not all women by all men. He understands too that someday he may be called upon to stop writing poetry and kill, and understands that this is not something he should understand. He is as sophisticated (I want to say) as this earnest young redhead is naïve; he is too like me. Him I understand, as I do his cadet counterpart on the other end of the spectrum; neither extreme poses a problem, the completely aware and the completely unaware.

It is all the others who stick in my craw; those caught between Athens and Sparta, about whom I think as I go jogging later in the cold, the upper surfaces of my hands feeling burned against the wind (I have packed without considering the difference between Maryland and New York temperatures), those more average cadets and midshipmen with their desire to do something honorable, right, and patriotic with their lives. Their drive, greater than that of the other high-average students in their high schools back in their hometowns, has brought them here and helps them endure the humiliations to which the system intentionally exposes them every day in its effort to teach them respect, the art of following orders, and team spirit.

But the respect taught at the Naval Academy is external, not my province of the internal. You salute the uniform because it has a stripe, or stripes, on it. Students are slapped down for questioning the decisions of superiors on the grounds that they have failed to "respect their rank," not that they have failed to respect the person.

This has made me think of the debate within the Catholic Church associated with the Donatist Heresy, over whether a priest, through sinful actions, could somehow lose the ability to function as a priest, lose the power to change the wafer into the Body of Christ and administer the sacraments in a binding manner. Islam faced similar challenges. The Church, like the military an institution that had to protect its viability, of course held to the doctrine of externals. How could it police a world in which the sacraments might suddenly become invalid because of something you couldn't see or determine? A priest might be sinful *qua* individual, the Church wisely held, but *qua* priest, he remained efficacious.

The military holds the same doctrine: we salute the uniform first and ask questions about the person inside it only much later. If pressed, military theorists would probably say there was supposed to be a correlation between the outward sign of rank and the person inside. But this would not be a necessary one. Of course an unlawful order need not be followed, but such extreme situations aside, orders must be obeyed not because the person is a good person, but because he or she is legally wearing the uniform.

I'm at the Academy to develop the insides of people; the institution in which I teach works primarily on their outsides. Sometimes these two things conflict.

I stop suddenly, my heart racing, my breath coming in foggy puffs, my exposed thighs seared by the cold air and almost scarlet. I am at the wall overlooking the narrow part of the Hudson. Behind me is the parade field, the ugly gray buildings. My hands grasp the sharp stones, their cold somehow more convincing than the cold of the air. Their solidity comforts me. Across the river, the trees flame red and gold.

Ship, Shipmate, Self

ONCE I AM back home from the poetry reading, life at the Academy goes on. The midshipmen do what they do to satisfy Mother B, the military side of things. And they do what they do to satisfy me. This semester, this means they go back to preparing their exercises for creative writing: sonnets, descriptions of a physical scene, explanations of an imaginary invention.

Many of them, however, write about their families. This is what they do best, perhaps because they are caught in a fragile in-between age close to graduation from college. After spending four years in an environment that discourages ongoing physical involvements between the men and women of the Brigade—sex in the Hall is forbidden, as is "fraternization" with a member of your own company, or an upperclass with a plebe—most of them, I believe, find contact with the opposite sex nasty, brutish, and short. After several years of collective lives in the dining hall and on the drill field it is, it seems, the warmth of their families at home that they remember most vividly, that situation in which they were each only one, rather than one-of-many, in small towns where they were usually the golden boy or girl of their year, in a time of youth and carelessness that seems to most of them like a vanished age.

Their ear for family dialogue is acute. I remember one student who read about squabbling in the back of the car on the way home from Midnight Mass on Christmas Eve. As he read out loud the insulting dialogue of the brothers in his narrative, he began to laugh, and later he broke into a smile over the responses of the mother, discovering as if for the first time through his own story how annoying his parents must have found his teenaged wisecracking.

Another student, a woman, read pages and pages of description of Sunday dinner in her Bronx Italian milieu, seen from the perspective of childhood: the scratchiness of an uncle's cheek as she kissed it, the smell of a great-aunt's hands, like that of the pink bottle of lotion on the windowsill. I told her that it needed shaping, and that she should think of writing a novel about her family: her knack for producing the filler of which our narratives are formed, with respect to her own memories, was (I told her) a real gift—all of the sights, sounds, he-saids and she-saids that make up the flesh of our stories and that she could, it seemed, churn out in endless profusion. Another student, speaking of her parents' marriage, which had not lasted, began to weep. I asked if we should go on to someone else and come back to her, but she shook her head, grimaced a smile through her tears, choked up again and, skipping a paragraph or two, lurched through the rest of her piece: it ended abruptly.

The Academy drills into its students a hierarchy of loyalties in which family doesn't even appear: ship, shipmate, self, in that order. Over and over again the students are told the scale of descending value. It's the Navy's version of the Latin motto *Non sibi, sed patriae*. Only the Navy puts a lump of hardware in place of the patria, the country or homeland. I can't say I'm completely comfortable with it. In creative writing, however, they are encouraged to focus on the self. Is this counter-"motivational"? A necessary outlet that helps the larger system run more smoothly? Do I feed or subvert the system? Which would be better?

Sometimes I come upon these same students from creative writing or those plebes I have in freshman English marching to the parade field in rigid company formation. On the Naval Academy grounds, automobiles must give right of way to ambulances, official cars, and midshipmen in formation. And so it sometimes happens that I sit in my car waiting for them to pass, or creep along behind them until they have abandoned the roadways and are back on the brick walks. Sometimes the ones I recognize are the ones running along beside the rigid ranks as overseers. They are free to wave at me. The others may not look to the side. So as not to make them feel that I am trying to tempt them into a forbidden response, I look away, pretending I have not seen them.

Recognizing them at all under their caps and in their uniforms when I see them anywhere outside of the classroom is an

acquired skill. The trick is to look at the eyes, focusing immediately, in the split second of approach before passing, on that
one narrow band of individuality—the face—that is exposed
through their otherwise identical clothing. After all these years,
I have gotten so good that I can recognize a midshipman with
the brim of his cover pulled down over his face. It is supposed to
come down to two-fingers-width from the bridge of the nose.
Sometimes one enters my class with an angry horizontal red line
across his or her forehead from the circular hatband inside; it
looks like a slash and makes the student seem oddly vulnerable.
Put on in the instant of exiting a building, by contrast, the caps
hide their eyes and render them daunting, like the mirrored sun-
glasses that give power to the motorcycle policeman.

I have never ceased to find it strange that these people toting
lead-filled rifles and clanking ceremonial swords so rigidly in
formation in the middle of the road are the same students who
sprawl at their absurdly undersized desks in my classes and reveal their dreams, their regrets, and their memories through
their written words. In the parades, the students' collective self
seems to congeal like an oil slick reflecting the sun, hiding any
glimpse of the life in the water below. And though the voice
from the reviewing stand gives the name and hometown of each
company commander as the company passes in review—which
suggests that each of these marching dots has a name and a place
of origin—from the stands, they are indistinguishable as individuals; only the women can be identified by their altered caps
and their shorter gaits.

There are more direct reminders to me of the life the midshipmen will ultimately lead, but they are brief: there are always those unsettling few days in the fall when the serenity of the campus is destroyed by the display of new military hardware manned by the Marines from across the river. Men in combat gear stand by the newest killing machines parked on the grass that leads to the chapel—the sacred grass that midshipmen may not walk on, so that the Yard does not become crisscrossed with the trails that gradually wear away the grass from a civilian college.

Most unsettling of all is seeing my students, who have just finished talking about Shakespeare, Brecht, or narrative structure, clustered around the displays, discovering how to camouflage themselves for polar warfare, talking animatedly to the equally enthusiastic Marines about hardware—from the latest howitzer to the serrated-edged knife for Navy SEALs. But then these barbed blobs of iron are removed from the grass, and things return to normal, with tourists and squirrels the only things allowed off the walkways.

Through all this, day in and day out, the structure of authority remains—and it is here that I taste most strongly the system my students are being trained to serve. I call the plebes by their last names: Mr. X and Miss Y. They call me "sir"; on the rare occasions when they think I am mad at them, the numbers of sirs in a sentence doubles, or trebles. I get what I want by telling them: could you please take your bookbag off the desk, I can't see you. They understand that this is an order. (Recently our building has been renovated, and the larger desks have disappeared; the current ones have stowable writing surfaces and are too small for bookbags: one problem solved. Indeed, now they are allowed to wear backpacks, rather than merely carry the "issue" bookbags. Some things do change.) When a student comes by during my office hour, he or she stands in the doorway and asks for "permission to come on board"; the student will not sit in the chair provided for that purpose until I explicitly invite him or her to do so. With the upperclassmen, I am looser, calling them by their first names. Yet here too I benefit from the system, because in the context of what they have come to expect, they sense this as a sign of personal interest, a sort of concession to be enjoyed.

My students better understand some of the things we read precisely because of the life they lead away from my eyes. They are more interested than most people in any text involving war, and I teach such texts more and more often in an attempt to involve them; they understand even better the texts that deal with power, with dedication, with responsibility. They understand structure better than do their contemporaries outside the Wall, and they understand the postponement of immediate pleasures in the pursuit of longer-term goals.

The thought of killing is something else they understand better than I, or at least appear to. At any rate, most of them seem to take it for granted. By contrast, I have not yet even come to terms with natural death—the cessation of that so-developed world of sensibility and feeling that literature exists to develop and preserve—much less death inflicted by one human being on another. How could someone live with the responsibility of having put an end to such a vast world as another human being? Yet most of them simply eat up the concoctions of blood, metal, and adrenaline that Hollywood produces. They root for the hero who mows down the enemy and cheer when he wins for his righteous cause. Or do they simply not understand the implications of what they are cheering for?

II

Owen at Annapolis

IN THE LAST weeks of the semester one spring, the trees pop with new life and the windows are open to the soft air. In the final class periods of plebe English (first semester: plays and short stories; second semester: poems and novels) we are reading World War I poets: Siegfried Sassoon, Rupert Brooke, and Wilfred Owen. I had thought myself daring for assigning these writers in an effort to discuss some ideas that are rarely brought up in my students' other courses—such as that war is not pretty, and that people can be hurt.

But this class period, as it turns out, goes differently than I had expected. I had intended to start with the imagery in "Disabled," a poem about a multiple amputee, and go on to "Dulce et Decorum Est," Owen's mordant response to Horace's assertion that "it is sweet and fitting to die for one's country" through a description of a gas attack. One student is waving his hand already. I have asked them to do some biographical research on these poets in preparation for a paper; I wonder if he has found something interesting.

He has. In fact, he bears the sensational news that Wilfred Owen, a decorated war hero killed in the trenches, was probably gay. There is stunned silence. "Why are you having us read gay poets?" several students, incensed at the news, ask. "Well," I say bravely to hide my exasperation, "I assigned them as war poets."

"But sir," they respond, "couldn't you have found us a normal poet?"

How could I have thrown overboard my careful months-long programming of poems about such macho subjects as motorcycles and straight sex to have poetry revealed, in these final weeks, as something riddled with gay men—as, in these early days of the 1990s, they fear their own Navy soon will be? Even for me, there are some topics that are simply not worth the time and trouble—and that would simply be traps, black holes into which the class's energy would pour without ever coming back. Better just to plough on, picking my way around the mines.

I take a deep breath. "Well," I say, "do you think that Owen's sexuality affected the poems?"

"No," says one of plebes. "Not in the poems we read."

"Right," I say, eager to get on, and for once asserting something rather than asking them what they think, "that seems to me the case too."

A few others nod their heads in agreement. I breathe more easily, but with a sense of bad faith. For in "Disabled," the young man who has lied about his young age to enter the military only to have his legs blown off is apparently straight, with a girlfriend named Meg. In "Dulce et Decorum Est" the men are so exhausted that sexuality never comes into question. And, I object silently to myself, a number of critics have maintained that Owen's imagery fairly drips with homoeroticism, and suggested that for Owen, part of the horror of war was that it killed off so many beautiful young men. Should I try to play devil's advocate against my own position, complicate the situation by suggesting that a poet's sexuality might not, in fact, be so easily separable from his art?

Mixed with my uncertainty as to how to proceed is my more immediate concern that the students not simply reject these poems out of hand because of the sexual orientation of their long-dead authors.

"As far as that goes," I say noncommittally, trying to cloud the issue, "there have always been gay men in the military. I mean, think of the Greeks."

A plebe in the back has an answer to that. "But sir," he says with great force, "Greece isn't a world power any more, is it?"

I am still sorting out the implications of that one when a plebe in the corner slowly raises his hand. He has read the same biographical sources on Wilfred Owen as the first questioner has, but he has a different view.

"Sir," he says hesitantly (it is clear that he is about to express an opinion he knows will be unpopular with his classmates), "I always thought that fags wouldn't kill anybody. I mean, I thought they were sort of fruitcakes. But Owen, he killed a lot of men. And he got a medal. It changed my views, reading that. I mean, he was okay."

"Interesting reaction," I say. Inside I am screaming. Being gay is clearly okay if you kill.

Should I object? Or, ever with an eye to the pedagogical edge, merely take what I am given?

"Sir," another says slowly, obviously emboldened by what his classmate in the corner has just said, "I mean, I don't know what anybody else thinks, but if it's a choice between a gay man with a rifle between me and the enemy and nobody at all, I'd rather have the gay man."

"Hmm," I say, trying to look professorial. "Do the rest of you feel that way?"

"Well, if you put it that way . . ." begins another.

"Yeah," says somebody in another row, "I've never thought of that."

I am saved—a discussion; I go into automatic and somehow make it through the hour. I squelch the momentary impulse to prepare them for Walt Whitman, our reading for the following week. You ain't seen nothin' yet, I think. Or should I just hope they don't see anything suspect in Whitman's obsession with manly love and his own hard root? Probably they won't, I think—it's too much like the language of the Naval Academy. And sure enough, at the next class they swallow Whitman whole and without complaint. Life is just far more complex than you know, I think.

These are the times of fulminating televangelists suggesting that AIDS is God's punishment for homosexuals. Their utter ignorance of a world outside the United States, such as AIDS-stricken Africa, where as many women are affected as men because their husbands sleep with (female) prostitutes, and where a whole generation of children is condemned to death from an inherited disease, infuriates and exasperates me. Still, many of the fulminators would point to my brother Keith as an example of what they mean. This knowledge exasperates me even more.

In the evenings and on the weekends, these waning months of 1991, I go and see my brother, who is gay (was gay? What does sexuality matter now?) and dying of AIDS. Keith was a cellist and earned a PhD in musicology. He specialized in musicologically informed performances of Baroque music, and as a musical contractor in the Washington area, he put together orchestras.

Though my sexuality turned out to be more standard than Keith's, I think I understand him. Keith dated no one in high school—nor did I, both of us young for our years, both of us unable to get a foothold in the hierarchical world of a small-town high school, which we found to be full of sound and fury and signifying, as we tried vainly and of course annoyingly to tell everyone at the time, pretty close to nothing.

Keith and I had the same body-denying childhood, so it doesn't surprise me that when he got physical, he went for it. I have memories of never having done anything physical with my father—not tussling, not running, not throwing a football, not weightlifting, not fishing. And we weren't going to learn to love physicality based on any outside influences either. Sports in our high school were the property of the lunks who thought Salisbury, Maryland, was the center of the world. My mother, from Albany via NYU, made sure we knew that it wasn't.

Keith told virulently anti-gay jokes almost up to the day he announced to me, as a response to a direct question—I can still hear the silence before he spoke, then the belligerent tone of his voice—that he was gay. I would guess he was celibate until his mid-twenties, when he was pulled out of the closet by the insistence of the personable young man who was his first lover. Michael ultimately left him because, he said, he couldn't stand Keith's promiscuity: Keith went from zero to ninety almost overnight. He was making up for lost time.

With respect to his appearance, too. For several years, Keith worked out relentlessly, taking the same revenge on his earlier body that I suppose I too continue to take, though perhaps in a more measured fashion. The result was that he popped his intentionally too-tight T-shirts, and, so I learned, went to leather bars to show off—and, I gather, to do other things. Taking charge of as many men as he could fit into his schedule would have been one way of proving to himself that he wasn't a nerd any more.

I can understand the need to take revenge on the past. What I don't understand is the logically unrelated fact of his apparently self-destructive attitude, toward AIDS among other things. I was far more interested in the subject than the average straight American at the time, because I lived and taught in the mid-1980s in Rwanda, epicenter of the epidemic, where HIV is supposed to have mutated from something in monkeys. I read voraciously on the subject before going to Africa; knowledge was nowhere near the current level. Back then, people weren't even completely sure the disease couldn't be transmitted by mosquitoes. I got a vaccine against hepatitis B because a French friend told me of new research linking it to AIDS. I knew enough to avoid prostitutes; almost 100 percent of them were infected.

Thus, returning home to visit from Rwanda, I asked Keith if he'd been tested for HIV. I had been, twice: a doctor at the embassy in Kigali, Rwanda's capital, had done it as a favor.

"What difference would it make?" he asked. And the conversation, he made clear, was over.

That was Keith in a nutshell. And then the belligerent stare, daring me to reopen a subject he had declared closed.

Two years before he died, Keith, my mother, and I made our annual theater trip to New York. My parents had divorced more than a decade before. Keith coughed so loudly in the Jerome Robbins revue we went to see the first night that people turned around and glared. The next day, he couldn't walk the two blocks to City Center and wanted to call a cab. I remember being impatient with him: It's only two blocks!

How could I have failed to realize what was going on?

Within days of our return he was in the hospital, diagnosed as HIV-positive. When he told me, I cried. He held up his leg, not noticeably different than before, but to him changed utterly, and made his flaccid calf muscle sway back and forth. "I'm wasting away," he informed me. "I'm dying."

"Not now," I said. "I mean, not right now." I'd talked to the doctor outside the room, who gave him two years. I repeated this to Keith, who didn't believe me. I got the doctor in to tell him.

The drugs and transfusions revived him for a time; he had another good year to play the cello and work on Gregorian chant. Then things began to unravel. For the last months of his life, his brain spiraling into dementia and his body now truly wasted away, prone to diarrhea and wracked by coughs, he lived on a cot in my mother's living room, waited on by her and tended by his faithful cat, who has now outlived him by more than a dozen years.

I would return from Keith to my students to find my pity for their youth gone, at least temporarily, and replaced with annoyance, especially after discussions like this one about Wilfred Owen. Some of them, after all, will certainly turn out to be gay. Like my brother, they're all acting as if they either aren't, or don't know it. Of course, I add immediately, what choice do they have at the Academy, which would "separate" them immediately if they announced the truth? And self-knowledge is hard-won. No one encourages the struggle at Annapolis.

Or maybe even elsewhere. I'm pretty sure Keith fought against being gay until he couldn't fight any longer, even denying the truth to himself. The fight made him very unhappy. Being gay wasn't for Keith a "choice" or a "lifestyle," as the right-wingers insist to my students—and as they repeat to me. Going to the leather bars: now *that* was a lifestyle. But that's actually the part I can almost understand. Who doesn't want to be found attractive after years of being told you're not?

Being gay and dying of AIDS are completely separate topics, though they were closely linked by fact in the West in the 1980s and 1990s. But before I could explain that to the midshipmen, I'd have to explain so many other things about human sexuality, and they probably wouldn't believe me about those things either.

Sex and Suits

GAY MEN AREN'T the only people who threaten the military nowadays. Women do too. One lieutenant in the English department told me about a situation on his prior assignment in which a male lieutenant was having an affair with a female lieutenant. It was quite legal, and the two didn't have to hide. So they didn't. The result, my young colleague told me, was that others' knowledge of the affair decreased the woman's ability to command men, knowing as they did that the male lieutenant was "banging" her every night. They'd look at her and snicker, all too able to visualize her with her legs spread. At the same time, it made the men resentful of the male lieutenant: he was getting some and they weren't.

All military institutions are by definition shrines to the Male. Military virtues are male virtues: hardness, toughness, strength, all of them derived from descriptions of desirable male secondary sexual characteristics, or simply references to tumescence. What, we might ask, of kindness, gentleness, and compassion? Any sailor worth his salt would immediately reject these as unmilitary, and identify them, correctly, as virtues at the Female pole.

For this reason, many of the same problems posed by gay men in the military are also posed by women. Currently, the Academy administration is on the politically correct side and brooks no discussion of the matter: we respect and value women at the Academy, we are told, and they are to be treated just like everyone else. But, I think, there is a difference between individual women and what Goethe called *"das ewig Weibliche"* and which we may call the Female, with its values and socialization patterns that may very well be different from those of the male. The Naval Academy may not reject women, but it does, largely, reject the Female.

The characteristic stances of the body required in the military are male, starting with that so-fundamental posture of rigid attention, with chest out and shoulders squared. It is both a position of subjugation (higher ranks do not come to attention for lower) and an offering of the body for aggressive use, where the fists can lash out to inflict harm on an enemy. It emphasizes the stillness and uprightness that are fundamental to male body language; women, by contrast, are freer to curve and move about.

Even clothing is Male. It is clear to anybody with eyes that military dress is made to flatter the male body. Navy suits for men, like male military uniforms the world over, are close-fitting, emphasizing the breadth of shoulders and minimizing the waist; the torso is further outlined by a **V** of gold buttons on their double-breasted coats. Starched shirts are held tight over chests and flat stomachs by a sort of garter belt, worn under the trousers, that links socks to shirttail, called a "shirt stay." Epaulets widen the shoulders even farther; the trousers of the Marines have scarlet stripes down the side (the "blood stripe") which function to call attention to and visually lengthen the leg. Women regularly grow swoony over men in Navy summer whites, which make skin tones stand out by contrast, and all men in both Navy and Marine Corps wear a cap whose inverted pyramid echoes in reverse the shape of the torso beneath and whose brim hides the eyes from the viewer, rendering the man underneath more menacing. A baseball cap that merely replicates the shape of the head does not have this effect, though it similarly shades the eyes, and I would submit that women wearing the reared-up military cover, as they do in some uniformed services and, for example, at the Air Force Academy, look as if they're playing dress-up. If we have any doubts that all this is meant to set off the male to best advantage, we should consider that uniforms look "right" on young men, whose bodies are the military ideal, and acutely embarrassing on older, out-of-shape men in a way that civilian clothing does not—as odd and finally sad as a seventy-year-old woman with dyed hair, a low-cut dress, and plenty of makeup.

Our students may be unaware of just how these things work, but they are extremely aware of looking good. They are constantly giving each other support by saying that someone looks "sharp," or, in a particularly high compliment, "like a stud." This does not mean he is particularly skillful with women. It only means other men think he looks nice. Indeed, all of this is about men dressing up for men. No wonder my students are such avid readers of *GQ*; no wonder they discuss my Italian suits and cannot seem to wrap their minds around the fact that my socks are never solid-colored, and, in my Left Bank affectation, sometimes lighter-colored than my suit.

In an institution as dedicated to looks as this one, they cannot fail to notice that the military uniform adapted for women is, at best, a compromise, and at worst a travesty. Certainly the women perceive their uniforms as unattractive; they speak derisively of their "birth-control shoes" and are aware that, as one female student told me, in her uniform she couldn't "look like a girl."

This failure of the female uniform is the result of what we might call structural factors. Close-cut clothing meant to free the male body for action ends up emphasizing its maleness; conversely, similarly functional clothing for women does not emphasize femaleness. This is so partly because the male, at least traditionally, defines his sexuality through doing, the female by being. We may not like this duality, and of course it is anything but absolute, but it is nonetheless a fact. Female uniforms go out of their way to deemphasize what is characteristic about the female figure, namely the breasts, in the same way the male uniform goes out of its way to emphasize what is characteristic about the male, the shoulders.

Ties, clearly too phallic to survive a trip across the gender gap unaltered, have been replaced in the female uniform by a coy little cross reminiscent of folded hands, whose primary function seems to be to refer to the tie that it replaces. Never has Freud's contention that a female is only a mutilated or imperfect male seemed so plausible as when looking at female military uniforms. But of course the uniforms are only an example of the belief, not a proof of its correctness. And what to make of the female Navy cap? It can have neither the inverted pyramid of the male (which rises in the front as if becoming erect—like the hood of a cobra, to which some men like to compare circumcised penises) nor the brim: what we get is pertly turned-up sides and a little bow at the back, all of which together convey none of the authority of the male and seem merely a placeholder for a "real" cover.

This question of how to feminize the clothing symbols of a male world is not a new one. It has been successfully addressed in the gender-mixed working world, and the solution has not been to have working women wear frilly party dresses. Attractive suits for female executives have been produced, combining an element of the feminine (usually a softening blouse with jewelry and stockings) with a shoulder-drape similar to that of male attire. This defines a female working attire because its complementary pole, the business suit, is less hypermasculine than male attire is in the military: no epaulets, no rows of buttons, no rising cap. Business clothing acknowledges the male figure without worshipping it; as a result, clothes for both men and women, though differentiated, are closer to a theoretical center.

What strikes me about the women in my English classes, where I am profoundly grateful for their presence because they render classroom discussion more normal, is how much "protective coloration" they adopt in the male-dominated world around them. This ranges from male body language—swinging their shoulders as they walk, straddling chairs—to the anti-female verbal language they use and the jokes they tell, that are just as sexist as anything a man could come up with.

One apparently shy woman surprised me by telling a joke (Friday was Joke Day; they looked forward to it) whose point was to list all of the orifices of a nun seeking entrance at the Pearly Gates that had been entered by a man. I was dumbfounded, wondering if she realized how worshipful of the male the joke was. The phallus conquers all, even vows of chastity, and does so as it likes. (She was the lone woman in the class, and rather good at standing up for herself. The day she was absent, however, the men seemed to let out their breath, and looked about them with great grins.) "He's not, like, whipped," another female student told me in class about Ibsen's blustering, hypocritical Torvald Helmer: not, that is, "pussy-whipped"; not under his wife's sway. I think she meant it admiringly.

Ultimately I had to abandon Joke Day: the jokes were getting too tasteless, and they betrayed such rampant fears and immaturities that I couldn't listen anymore. The contrast between their well-scrubbed, nice-looking exteriors and the confusion inside was too upsetting for me to bear. Many of the jokes were anti-female, which I wasn't about to be condoning by silence— and I could hardly jump down their throats for an inappropriate joke when I'd encouraged them to tell a joke in the first place. Then there were the eternal gay jokes, as if the usual percentage of men here wouldn't turn out to want sex with men rather than with women. Then there were the anal- and oral-sex jokes that so clearly showed their fascination with these forbidden things.

Women's Head

THIS GRAFFITO, IN an otherwise pristine men's toilet stall in Sampson Hall, stayed up several days before it was found and removed:

WOMEN SHOULDN'T BE HERE. I KNOW IT. YOU KNOW IT.
WHY DO WE REMAIN SILENT? TELL A WOMAN TO LEAVE!

In an institution that rejects, insofar as it can, the Female, how will females ever truly fit in? The outlook seems grim. If it's not the constant criticisms of the female midshipmen (they're ugly, they're fat, they get preferential treatment), it's some new story about a rape in the Hall that went unreported. At the Air Force Academy, this has finally blown up into a full-bore scandal, with heads rolling, and people being shocked, *shocked* that something like this goes on. If it's happening at Colorado Springs, it's happening at Annapolis too.

Recently I realized that I hadn't heard any anti-female gibes in a while. I wondered if my sense that women were excluded from the mainstream life at the Academy—except when the powers-that-be chose women for leadership positions: See? We're not sexist! The Brigade Commander is a woman!—was exaggerated.

I decide to ask my students. The next day I do. A plebe raises his hand to answer my question. It's the end of the semester, and they know I let them say forbidden things.

"My company officer," he tells us, "says he can't respect a shipmate who can't do as many push-ups as he can. Where does that leave women?"

I always make it a point to find an excuse to "drop" in one of the early sessions and pound out twenty plyometric (clapping) push-ups followed by as many more as I can pump out: I can do between forty-five and fifty, and it never fails to impress them. I know the power of the push-up at Annapolis.

"Women have a raw deal at the Naval Academy," I insist.

"But sir," they erupt. And I get a thousand stories at once of women being pushed into leadership positions they shouldn't have, of unfair breaks given to students because they're women, of how women don't have to do pull-ups but only arm-hangs, and have an easier version of the O (obstacle) course.

"Let's ask the women here," one male student says.

It's a class of eighteen men and two women, and of course I'm not going to embarrass the women by making them "speak for their sex." "That's not fair," I say.

"Please, sir!" they beg.

I give up and turn to the two women, who tend to sit together. "Ladies?" I ask, holding up my hands to show they don't have to take the bait if they don't want to.

The male student with the push-ups isn't ready to let them talk. "They had to know what they were getting into," he insists.

This is as good a lead-in as any other. I turn again to the women. "Did you?" I ask.

"No," says one, as if I'm asking a silly question.

"I had no idea," says the other.

I bet they didn't. I've seen our adrenaline-pumping PR movies, heard the officers who represent the Academy in geographically far-flung places talk the place up as if it's a combination of Camelot and a toy store. Reality doesn't have much of a chance.

150 Years of Leadership, Service, and Academics

FOR THE ACADEMY'S sesquicentennial year of 1995, the gates were festooned with colorful banners. The banner over the gate by Herndon reads: 1845–1995: 150 YEARS OF LEADERSHIP, SERVICE, AND ACADEMICS WITH A VISION OF THE FUTURE.

The military has always known that men fight not for principles, but for other men. Why else does the word "leadership" come first in the banner over Gate 3? Men die for their platoon leader, a young lieutenant with fire in his eyes, not for the President back home in Washington, or the ideals of democracy—or for that matter the ideals of fascism, or whatever the prevailing national ideology might be.

Because sex—or as we say nowadays, gender—is such an important part of military self-definition, men in combat can identify easily only with another man, trying to compete with him and live up to his ideals. Thus male bonding is still at the center of the Academy. Our male students know it, but, in our attenuated gender climate, are not allowed to say it. Our female students come to learn it; their complaints are treated as isolated incidents rather than as evidence of structural flaws.

Male bonding is socialization not only in the absence of the Female (if not in the absence of women), but also to a certain extent through rejection of the Female (which tends to mean through rejection of women). It implies not only the denigration of the Female, but the worship of the Male. And this means that it is profoundly homoerotic. The paradox of the Academy is, therefore, that it is both homoerotic and homophobic—and perhaps the second because of the first.

Many intense relations between straight men are homoerotic, because they are single-sex and invariably physical. Heterosexual men feel the need to make contact with one another's bodies, even though they usually do so by crashing into one another rather than caressing. They even trade body fluids—sweat and blood rather than semen. T-shirt seen in the gym: "He who sheds his blood with me is my brother." The reference is to battle, though the shirt is put out by the rugby team. (GIVE BLOOD, PLAY RUGBY, reads the bumper sticker.) Straight men even cry together. Indeed, men who have cried together, as under moments of great emotion or stress, tend to stick together, perhaps because they are ashamed of having done so.

Male bonding is physical bonding. You can talk at another guy forever and leave him cold. Wrestling with him, especially if you win, makes him your buddy for life. Afterward you downplay your victory and buy him a beer.

A year or so ago, I went swimming in one of the Academy pools one Saturday afternoon. Only a few people were there, churning out their laps. Among them was a muscular young man trying, somewhat haplessly, to do the crawl, as I became aware out of the corner of my goggles after a few laps. As I was about to flip at the wall, I saw him hanging on the end, waiting to interrupt me. He did so with the naïve impoliteness of midshipmen toward each other: it is assumed that any one will help another at any time.

"Can you help me with this freestyle?" he said. Then suddenly, I was aware, the pieces reconfigured before his eyes, and he saw his English professor rather than another buffed-up guy in goggles and a Speedo. His eyes widened. In about the same moment, I recognized him as a student who had been giving me problems all semester: by nature not a gifted writer, he was clearly among those who thought that English class here at a military institution is a waste of time.

"Hi, Mr. Carter," I said, as affably as I could. In fact, I was a bit miffed at having been interrupted. Besides, I didn't really like him. "What can I do for you?"

"Sir," he says. "Sir, excuse me."

"No problem," I say, consciously lapsing into the vernacular to put him at his ease. "What's up?"

He hesitates, then decides to go on.

"Well, sir," he says, "I'm having trouble with my swimming exam. I noticed you just swimming along and I thought maybe, before I knew it was you, you could help me."

"Sure, Mr. Carter," I say.

We have a swimming lesson. Fingers together, pointer in

water first, S-curve, kick from the hips. First we try it in the pool. He doesn't get it, jackknifes his body. We climb out, and, standing on the edge, I show him how to do the crawl, and then the breaststroke. Echoes of the countless swimming lessons when I was ten come back to me: pull, breathe, kick, glide.

He gets in and tries, but keeps buckling at the waist and failing to bring his feet together. I jump in, grab his ankles, and force him to do it right. His body understands what his mind did not. Five minutes later he is thanking me, and I resume my laps.

The next day in class, he is a different person. Suddenly respectful and no longer sneering, he shows himself to be a model, if not particularly strong, student, making a real effort and, in fact, as the semester draws to a close, getting better. He liked me, and probably as a result, I liked him. Until he graduated I crossed paths with him occasionally; he always seemed genuinely pleased to see me.

All I had to do to get his respect was to be better than he was at something physical. And also to show him my pecs. His were better, I can say generously, like slabs of raw liver jutting out from his body. But he couldn't swim. Besides, he's shorter than I am, my V-taper is better, and, being the professor, I'm the one in the power position. I still have the testosterone advantage.

One spring day, I'm wearing a short-sleeved shirt and equally short-sleeved linen summer jacket I thought was funky.

First, they note the jacket. "Lookin' sharp, sir," they tell me.

The jacket is discussed. Abruptly and with no particular embarrassment, a male student speaks up: "Sir, pull up your sleeve and flex for us."

"Don't be silly," I say, surprised by their directness.

The chorus becomes general. "Oh, sir," they plead, "please."

"For heaven's sake," I say. Of course, I am not a little flattered.

I pull up my sleeve and flex.

"Hoo-ya!" they scream. "Huge, sir!"

"Double-barreled!" one pleads. In for a penny, in for a pound, I think.

For this I have to take off my jacket. I do. The sudden silence is thick enough to cut. I flex both arms at once.

They erupt again. "Look at those guns!" they yell, delighted.

I grin to accept the compliment, put my jacket back on, and get back to *Madame Bovary*.

When they have calmed down, they listen that much more intently, it seems, to what I have to say about poor abused Emma. Biceps are good for something around here, and it has nothing to do with impressing women.

Usually I am amused by their overwhelming infatuation with Maleness, a shrine at which I too worship. At the same time, as a man who loves women, I find it stifling. In my more desperate moments, I want the giant, phallic Herndon statue replaced with an enormous female nude, a Venus of Willendorf, and the exercise to be one of licking hundreds of pounds of honey from her breasts and haunches. Women need not participate, and indeed may continue to do homage to the obelisk, like modern-day bacchantes. Such a suggestion, if made seriously, would certainly be perceived as harassment and cause for severe official reprimands, while its male equivalent is a cherished part of "tradition."

I think of something a student said a few years back, a young man who, because he was an English honors candidate, I saw nearly every day. One evening the class had a makeup session at my house: we ate popcorn and listened to the embalmed voice of T.S. Eliot, all dying falls and Ds for Ts, read *The Waste Land*. A couple of students stayed to help me with the dishes. In the course of the conversation, I made a comment about misogynistic attitudes in Eliot and at Annapolis.

Randy looked first at his friend, then at me. The three of us were alone in the suddenly silent kitchen.

"Sir," he said, deciding it was okay to say what he was thinking, "I don't tell this to everybody. But I don't think women should be at the Naval Academy. It's a male thing. It's the brotherhood. I'd die for the guys in my company. We share everything."

He laughed to minimize his intensity. "Heck," he said, "we'd even share women. We'd share . . ." He trailed off, looking for an example stronger than women. "We'd share each other's jockstraps!" he said, and both guys laughed in agreement.

"Well," Randy added abruptly, hanging up his towel, "gotta go. Thanks for the evening, sir."

They left me thinking of a long line of twenty-one-year-olds, linked together by nothing less fundamental than the sweat of their balls. Young men joined at the crotch: how remarkable this image seems to the outsider, and how normal here at USNA.

Each year I discuss with my students the fact that on Induction Day, they have raised their right hands and sworn to uphold not the superintendent of the U.S. Naval Academy or their immediate commanding officer, not even the commander-in-chief in Washington, but something much more abstract: the United States Constitution. A tall order for anyone, I think, to be willing to die to support principles; still, this is what they have sworn.

Against this is the fact that the "leadership" we claim we're trying to foster means getting men to do things they don't want to do—getting them to do these things for *you*, not for a principle. The more clear-eyed officers, who are intelligent men and women, discuss precisely such paradoxes. It seems to have little effect. How demeaning that the military, so full of its own virtues, should in the last analysis be only the tool of politicians, mere civilians! And to have as commander-in-chief a man like Bill Clinton, whose military past consisted of protesting against involvement in Vietnam—what a bitter pill.

No wonder they feel that happy days have returned again in the person of George W. Bush, who says the right things despite whatever he may have done or not done. The military prizes public actions, like the Pledge of Allegiance, and the noontime prayers to God in the dining hall that are being challenged by the American Civil Liberties Union and are just as hotly defended by the administration. The point isn't what you believe inside, but the act of publicly giving support to something. External public action being the currency of the military, what the President does and says is good enough.

Military as Victim

LIKE THE HOMOSEXUAL subculture, the military constitutes a marginalized subgroup in our society. And it's afflicted with some of the same resentments of mainstream society. From the outside, places like Annapolis look like bastions of privilege. From within, however, they seem fragile places indeed, fraught as they are with defensiveness regarding the admittedly subsidiary place of the military in a democratic society.

The military, in my experience, feels almost universally that it was not allowed to do its job in Vietnam. This, of course, is the only reason the United States can have lost. Our students resent the politicians who purportedly hamstrung military efforts as well as the protesters who finally helped bring the war to an end. When we discuss the Vietnam conflict, all they want to talk about is their firm belief that "Sir, they spit on the veterans!" and how wrong it was that the people back home for whom the troops were ostensibly fighting didn't "support" them. It's useless for me to explain that the distinction is fine between supporting *individuals* and supporting their uniforms, actions, or personal beliefs as well. What is left to support when all of these things are subtracted? To them, it seems unfair: if troops fight, citizens should at least cheer them on. Life is like a great football game; at Annapolis, after all, they are required to attend football games and cheer. The military always feels wounded when civilians don't "support the troops." After all, they protest, we're doing it for you!

In fact, the military is its own end. Many of those in the military see it as a purer, better place than the world outside, the world of "civilian scum,"; a place where honor and duty count for something, and by the way, a place where men can be men. The military acts rough and tough, but actually it's quite thin-skinned.

As a Navy captain at new-faculty orientation when I arrived said, quoting a song, midshipmen are the "pampered pets of Uncle Sam," paid to attend college, with a roof over their heads, clothing on their backs, food three times a day for which they have only to show up, their laundry done, and dozens of mother-hen handlers fussing around them, from their company officers to the deans. Yet the midshipmen see themselves, surprisingly to the outside world, as the most put-upon of human beings, their freedoms circumscribed, their weekends and summers prescribed, and their duties causing them to miss out on the beer parties of what they call "real schools" and a standard adolescent social life.

Further feeding the local sense of resentment may be the fact that the service academies in general and Annapolis in particular are not taken as seriously as their leaders would like by university types along the Harvard/MIT/Chicago/Stanford axis. Because these administrators are not academics themselves, they frequently have a hard time understanding why this is the case. I have known people at the University of Chicago Club meetings, to which I used to go sporadically, laugh openly when I tell them I teach at Annapolis.

"It isn't really education, now is it?" one woman said with a sneer.

"Yes," I answered, annoyed. "It's really education."

Still, I went off feeling that I had let my dislike of the woman herself color my answer. Is it education?

Much of what we do, I had to concede silently and after the fact, is training, the conservative's version of education. At Annapolis, we are unashamedly in the business of cleaning up our students, in their actions as well as their appearance, making gentlemen (and now ladies?) out of students who may not be such when they arrive. Since few students when they arrive anywhere fit this bill nowadays, and since other institutions have long ago abdicated this role, our students may come out looking better in the end. Or at least, better insofar as surface manners are concerned.

Their "sir"s and "ma'am"s already make them by definition more polite than the vast majority of their peers, even if these courtesies are learned by rote and by compulsion. Yet I've learned the hard way that the fact they have to greet certain people this way means they resolutely refuse to greet anyone else in this manner. If I walk across the campus in a teaching outfit—a suit, with my Department of the Navy ID tag prominently displayed—midshipmen I cross will invariably greet me with the learned-by-rote "Good morning, sir" or "Good afternoon, sir." With the ID gone, I lose about half; with the tie gone, say on a non-teaching work-in-my-office day, almost all will look the other way. They can tell I'm not in their "chain of command." Why bother? Perhaps more to the point, they take revenge on what they do have to do by eliminating even common politeness when they aren't required to exhibit it.

On Friday nights, I sometimes see them walking about campus in their "mess dress," tight waiter-tops with gold cummerbunds for the men, long skirts for the women: they are going to or coming from a "dining in," where they dine formally in company and are taught some social graces. Not a bad idea for anyone, I sometimes think: and at what civilian institutions are there still teas or garden parties? There were the latter at Bryn Mawr in my time, but I suspect they've gone the way of all such things in the civilian world.

In their "pro" (short for professional) book, on which they are quizzed by the upperclass students, facts about battleships alternate with the information that in polite society, a gentleman pulls out a chair for a lady. At Annapolis, they still practice eating formal meals. Where else is that true? Elsewhere, the notion that the institution takes on the role of the parent is dead as a dodo. But dodos of this sort are everyday sightings at Annapolis.

Better than these surface manners, of course, would be a more ingrained politeness and an intrinsic set of societal rules, the "inner-directed" gyroscope, to use David Riesman's metaphor from his 1950s classic *The Lonely Crowd* for what keeps someone going who relies on his or her internal set of values. Maybe then there would be greetings for those on the walks not wearing a tie.

By Honor Bound

IN 1994, THE first wave of scandals hits. It has become clear that our superintendent will retire under a cloud. I can't feel too sorry for him. He's too hail-fellow-well-met for my taste, too much the good-ol'-boy, back-slapping jock. What has done him in is his unwillingness to believe that "his boys," the members of the football team, could have participated in what is clearly a massive night-before dissemination of an illicitly-procured electrical engineering exam. He himself is a former USNA football team co-captain.

Apparently the players thought both that they deserved the answers, and that they could get away with it. Yet what, I wonder, is so surprising about this? The football team here is fed separately in order to let them bulk up, worshipped at pep rallies, where the students go crazy and let off steam, and held up for emulation as the spearheads for Academy "spirit" in that annual battle with the Enemy, the Army-Navy game. Of course, all that coddling has led the football team to think they are invincible and would continue to be coddled. No wonder the Admiral declared the investigation closed and announced to a hall full of disbelieving midshipmen that no members of the football team were involved. A shouting match erupted among the incredulous midshipmen, and with that the scandal broke. Soon the Naval Criminal Investigative Service (CIS) was called in.

Ultimately, about half the football team turned out to be involved, along with others. After the full extent of the scandal was uncovered and the superintendent was widely known to have been remiss in failing to pursue it, the man himself sat in our English department library with his huge hands between his legs and confessed, despairingly, "I just didn't believe they could do it." The cheating scandal occurred "on his watch," which meant he was going to pay. At any rate, the findings of the investigation were that if he did not actually hush it up, he certainly did not investigate it aggressively.

He seems a bit bewildered, and has the air of a broken man. His career—everyone knows—is effectively over; he is an embarrassment to the Navy. He appears shell-shocked, waiting out his time. There are rumors that he will retire just after graduation, and the rumors prove true.

When asked by the Naval investigators why they did not turn in known cheaters, our students invariably said they would not rat on a classmate. After all, midshipmen are constantly told, Don't bilge on classmates. Given any contest between abstract principles and the concrete individual, individuals win every time: that's the paradox of the military. It claims it's more honorable than the outside world; in fact it's only more loyal. Its loyalty is to individuals, not principles. Now, all of a sudden, we were throwing principles at them: I can see why they would be confused.

They were confused for other reasons. The rules of the Honor Concept are so numerous and the actions they regulate so omnipresent that the midshipmen learn to constantly take shortcuts. The absolute size of the infraction is unimportant: if someone can be dishonorable in a minor affair, he or she can be equally so in a major one. An honor infraction, in this sense, is kin to a religious sin: there are greater and lesser offenses, but all are sins. Dishonorable is dishonorable, like a bacterium that taints an entire sample.

A student of mine tells a story on herself: though aware of the rule that midshipmen may remove only one piece of fruit from the trough in King Hall, she walked away with a bunch of bananas. When questioned, she tells me ruefully, she gave as her explanation that she was taking only one piece. A bunch is joined together, no? "Okay," she is told. She continues victorious, but with a bad conscience, she tells me. She knows that this is not the spirit of the rule, but only the letter. Yet in an institution where the letter is so often used to punish, why should she not, for once, take advantage of it?

Unlike the internal notion of sin, however, the Honor Concept applies only to actions. Historians sometimes evoke E.R. Dodds' distinction between what Dodds called "shame" and "guilt" cultures, exemplified by, respectively, Classical and Christian cultures. In a shame culture, demerits are external.

Both praise and blame are understood to be public concepts. A guilt culture, by contrast, demands that the individual give him- or herself praise or blame, even if as the result of public prompting. Only people in a guilt culture are "inner-directed," to use another of Riesman's terms.

The Naval Academy is a shame culture set in a larger guilt culture, its demerits based on things done rather than things thought. If you do X, Y, or Z, then you lack honor, and men/women with honor cannot associate with you and will never be able to trust you. How, I wonder, can people who are constantly told what to do develop their own inner gyroscopes?

The system promises the worst for all offenses, and in many cases, frequently for apparently arbitrary reasons, metes out a less-draconian punishment. Despite what the students are told, separation is not the only possible outcome of a guilty verdict. Frequently, offenders are counseled rather than even being tried, but if they are tried and found guilty, many are now subjected to "honor remediation" and restriction to quarters rather than being kicked out. The final call in any case is made by the Commandant or the Admiral, and hence it is extremely variable.

The students are acutely aware that for every person caught and punished, there are a dozen who are never caught and several handfuls who are caught but not punished. The current political climate determines much concerning what infractions are punished, and how severely; other factors, reportedly, are how the Admiral feels about you; what your skin color is (with the system eager to retain nonwhite students, gossip suggests that rules are bent for midshipmen of color); and how influential your parents are: in short, the factors that play roles in the outside world's judgments as well. Perhaps this is not such a bad thing. In fact, students sometimes tell me that the Academy is a very good training for life outside it. "Sir," they say, "if you can put up with the bullshit here, you can put up with it anywhere." Is this our intention, to create a trial by bullshit? To prepare students for the arbitrary nature of the world by exemplifying it here to the tune of $250,000 per student?

With respect to our cheating scandal, the perception is that equity has been very badly served. The Yard is buzzing with recent examples of people thrown out for what seem minute infractions of the rules: misrepresenting one's presence or absence at roll call, misstating one's weight on a report, or using someone else's ID card in a town bar. At the same time, known cheaters are being retained, shown leniency. Students are telling me that the system has been unfairly applied: those who confessed are being separated, those who continued to lie are being retained; children of important people are being protected. Maybe the argument that this is reality training has some merit. But then, what has become of the Camelot promised them by their Blue and Gold officers—local liaisons to the admissions board—and their own overactive idealism?

Elvis and Törless

ONE BOOK THAT would help all our students, I think, is Robert Musil's early novel *The Confusions of Young Törless,* set in a pre–World War I Austro-Hungarian military school. The eponymous hero is possessed by the desire to understand a craven classmate with a distinctly non-German name, one Bazzini, who had stolen and thus Done Wrong: Törless hopes to taste this (to him) so-solid thing, Dishonor. His world's emphasis on Honor suggests to him that there must exist an equally substantial shadow world that finally has come within his grasp. Törless's desire to understand the thief takes the form of torturing him and then subjecting him to sadomasochistic homosexual acts: part of the victim's degradation is that he submits, it appears, willingly (he's afraid of being exposed as a thief), and for a time Törless is convinced that he has, in consorting with Bazzini, in fact experienced Evil.

What Törless ultimately discovers, however, is that there is no Wrong, no realm of inky blackness into which those who have acted dishonorably descend, no taste of Evil. Bazzini is simply craven, a person like any other except with considerably less self-respect, ultimately uninteresting and not worth the hero's time.

Evil does not exist, only people who act in a certain way; here Törless comes to the same conclusion as did Hannah Arendt some decades later, with her famous theory of the "banality of evil." The specific case Arendt was considering was that of Adolf Eichmann. What struck Arendt was that this master of evil was fundamentally boring: banal, without thought. Thinking in and of itself, she proposed, obviated evil, at least of this sort: reflective people, which is to say people who are conscious of others and of the effects of their own actions, cannot by definition act as Eichmann acted.

That spring of 1994, I find out what cheaters look like. Like Törless, I discover that they look like everybody else. One day, a student vaguely reminiscent of a young Elvis, who had stopped handing in any work about a month before, knocked on my office door. (Shortly after the beginning of the class one day, he had told me in a cheerful-sounding but possibly also rueful fashion that he didn't "have a creative bone in [his] body." As time went on, I began to agree with him.)

"Hello, sir," he says, sticking his head around the edge of the door. "I just wanted to let you know why I haven't been turning in work."

"Have a seat," I say affably, putting a finger in my book. He sits. I swivel my chair around. "I'm under investigation in the cheating scandal," he tells me.

I look at him, trying to appear blasé. Secretly I am both fascinated and appalled, as if he had told me that he liked having sex with pigs. "Oh," I say. Then feeling dangerous, I add, "Did you cheat?"

"Yes, sir," he tells me with no particular embarrassment. "I'm not happy about it," he adds immediately, evidently aware that he is supposed to say something, "but that's the way things are."

"Will you be separated?" I ask, trying to stick to the administrative side of things.

"I don't know, sir," he answers with a grin. "They're still deciding. I'm going to start doing the work just in case I can stay. Otherwise I'm transferring."

"To where?" I ask, I hope pleasantly.

"Penn State," he says.

His manner is still cheerful; he says he has "come to terms with the situation." His parents are upset, and all he wants is for it to be over, for a decision to be made. He is tired of waiting to hear. Of course, he adds, it isn't fair.

I wonder suddenly what he has been thinking all semester: I have occasionally let drop a derogatory comment or two about the cheaters. How stupid of me not to realize that some of the students whose work I tried so hard to be positive about might well be involved. I feel a flash of regret, worried that I will have upset them. But how concerned should I be about their feelings? He himself cheerfully admits guilt and yet hopes to be retained. His biggest complaint is that others are being shown mercy while he may not.

Furthermore, two of his buddies, who sit beside him in my class, are in the same situation. "Sir," he asks, "did you notice the way John shaved his head last week?" I have thought nothing of it and have made no comment. A male shaved head is not an unusual sight at the Naval Academy: those who choose Marine Corps in the spring Service Selection have their heads shaved for them, and sometimes the haircuts they get are virtually indistinguishable from a head-shaving. Having no hair at all is called having a motivational haircut.

"That was in protest," he tells me.

"Protest?" I ask, puzzled.

"Well, sir, you know, against the investigation and so on."

How many of those implicated are there sitting in front of me three days a week, in this group of people whose attention and interest I try so desperately to engage? I don't want to be defended by scumbags like you, I think.

And, I add mentally, I don't want scumbags like you on the face of the Earth. But that one I'll leave to a higher authority. I think of a T-shirt one of the Marines has been wearing in the gym: KILL 'EM ALL: LET GOD SORT 'EM OUT.

What have I become, liberal me with my Quaker education and my nuanced "yes-but" reaction to everything? When push comes to shove, I find I have absolutely no tolerance for willful flouting of the rules. Mistakes are forgivable. This was no mistake.

Two days after Elvis's announcement, I get a visit from the shortest boy in the class. Since then I have found out that he is the class president; I can only assume there is some sort of "mascot" mentality at work here, as the mids usually choose a strapping achiever they are all proud of as their president.

Shorty has come by to tell me some news. Elvis's visit has primed me.

"Uh, sir," he says. "I'm being separated. You know, the cheating thing."

"How do you feel about that?" I ask, to avoid reacting.

He is, he says, resentful that others have done worse and are being retained, and he suspects that he is being held to a higher standard because he is the class president. "I feel good about myself," he ends, somewhat defensively.

He is a likable fellow. He speaks about his family, who own a clothing store, about how proud they were that he made it to the Naval Academy. He is optimistic about the future, dealing with adversity in a positive way. In some sense, he is behaving in an admirable fashion. How, after all, is he to live with himself? He admits his mistake and wishes that it had come out differently.

By now my mind is elsewhere. I am thinking of Joe, who usually sits next to Shorty in class. Joe is a hard-bitten blond boy with a buzz cut and stubby fingers. He is working-class Polish. His creative efforts are moderately interesting and unabashedly patriotic. He writes about his dreams to serve his country, expresses his knowledge that he will never be the top of the heap academically, talks of having kept at it "no matter what." His father, dead in Vietnam, is his inspiration.

Joe is painfully prudish: on those occasions when a work we are analyzing seems to be about sex, he turns beet-red because there are a handful of women in the classroom. He is hulking; I would not like to be on the receiving end of his ire.

Joe tried for several years to get into the Naval Academy before succeeding, I have learned from one of his pieces; virtually everything he writes is autobiographical. It had been his lifetime dream. By dint of hard work, he has been just over the passing line for his entire four years. Still, he passed electrical engineering, the course that occasioned the scandal, and he did so honestly. His confidence in the system, he writes, was first shaken by seeing how favoritism was shown to some of the cheaters. According to Joe, they should all be out.

One day a few weeks before, I saw Joe in the hallway. He slowed down as if to talk to me.

"Hi, Joe," I said.

"Hello, sir," he said, clearly having something on his mind. I saw him hesitate. I waited. "Sir," he said finally, "I just wanted to let you know I appreciated what you said."

"What I said?" I asked, puzzled. I say a lot of things.

"You know, sir," he said. "About the cheaters and how you disapprove. I think you and I see eye-to-eye on things. It made me feel good to hear you say what you said."

"Maybe I should have kept my opinions to myself," I said.

"Oh, no, sir," he insisted.

He was right. Whatever the personal consequences for those affected, I should be standing up for my—and his—principles. The Academy's principles, those unalterable, core values that are so easy for me to relativize in the abstract and so difficult to avoid in the particular.

Stupidly, standing there with Joe, who had told me so much about himself in his papers, I suddenly felt close to tears.

"I'm rooting for you, Joe," I told him, and I meant it.

I was glad that Joe was my student. I felt like giving him a bear hug and pounding him on the back, or tackling him with a whoop to show my affection. If I had been his classmate, I could have. But I was the professor, and above such exhibitions. Instead, I shook his hand, hard, and wished him well.

Just about the time I am ready to say that what we ask of our students is too much, I run into somebody like Joe. Yet probably I should not be concluding too much from the existence of people like Joe. He's too much like me, an army of one. Joe wants to be a Marine. He will make a fine one, alone with his wits on a deserted beach or lost in the jungle.

Mrs. Helmer and Mrs. Woolf

OTHER STUDENTS HAVE other problems. One young woman, whom I like immensely because she writes loopy poetry and would have done well as a late-sixties flower child, feels, she has told me on numerous occasions, that she cannot develop here. "The choices are too easy," she tells me. "They tell us what to do, we do it. Where's the growth in that?"

I try to help her think through the implications. She's considering transferring (they may transfer during the first two years without penalty) to the Seven Sisters school she turned down to come to us. She has other options, and I'm not too worried about her. Ultimately, she decides to stay. She goes into the Marine Corps.

In the case of another young woman in the same class with more casual thoughts of leaving, I am sure of what to recommend: she should stay. The bitter fact is, she doesn't have so many options, being somewhat older, black, and not from a wealthy family—she came to us from the fleet. And her problems aren't as serious.

She is not found aggressive enough and is consistently graded lower than anyone else on "performance" in her company. "Sure," she tells me, "I could get the plebes up at oh-six-hundred for a PEP run. The people who write my fitrep would like that. But the plebes wouldn't. It would be selfish."

She is bright and articulate, and she writes well. Yet she doesn't understand what she would be giving up by leaving.

"Think about it," I tell her. "As a woman, especially a black woman, you'll immediately get a lot of respect if you can tell people that you graduated from Annapolis. Take my word for it: it's money in the bank."

"Really?" she asks. Her surprise is genuine. For a moment her face is mistrustful, then it clears.

"I see what you mean," she tells me. "You mean how people perceive me, not who I am."

"Yes," I tell her. "How people perceive you." She too stays.

Their problems are minor compared to those of the slight young man with dark hair, also in the same class, who, I know, has been applying to Ivy League schools since mid-semester. For several months I have wondered what is going on with him. When we hit the Modernists in our Western Literature II course, he began to produce violent polemics in place of the analytical papers I had asked for. Obviously, the expression of the marginalized, and the power of that marginalized to make itself canonic through sheer force of words, that define Modernism, is deeply troubling to him.

Not one of the great strapping boys with their easy sexism and ear-to-ear grins in which this institution abounds, he is quiet, rather small, and, I thought, inoffensive. Why, I wonder, is this young man rising to the defense of the patriarchy, the system? Why his violent rejection of the actions of Nora, heroine of Ibsen's *A Doll's House,* who leaves her hypocritical and lying husband so she can find herself? For when he gets to Ibsen, he tears Nora apart: she should have stayed, no matter what. How could she leave her children?

I content myself with asking, in the margin of his paper, if he did not agree that Helmer, Nora's husband, was a complete failure as a human being, and a liar to boot. How could Nora have gotten him to admit the truth if she had stayed? As soon as Helmer is out of danger, he resumes his mantle of blustering control and attempts to silence her. At the very least, I'd like some acknowledgment from this young man that this is in fact Ibsen's view; I have seen none. I write this too in the margin.

My reaction produces the young man himself for the first time. He sits in my office and talks to me of things he has evidently been worrying about all semester. He claims he has limited time, but ends up staying three hours; when I leave, it is well past dinnertime and the sky is nearly dark outside. The longer he talks, the more clearly I see in him the bitterness of the disappointed lover: he is now defending at all costs a system in which he no longer believes, playing out a futile attempt after the fact to create something he could, or perhaps should, have believed in. He tells me he has come to us from the Jesuits, in whose system he also came to disbelieve over time. Annapolis was clearly meant to replace the Church; he is incensed now that it has not done so. What is left to guide him after the failure of the Church and the military to do so?

It will take some doing for this boy to retrace his steps, I think; to withdraw from his somewhat desperate commitment to this institution. He had put on a big push to come to Annapolis, talking his way in over the initial medical rejection of the board due to his asthma. In reply, he challenged any member of the board to run five miles with him: despite his condition, he competed in track and field. Impressed by such tenacity, the board relented. Now he is in the embarrassing position of finding that he does not want the thing he had fought so hard to attain. His reaction is to assert the more loudly: it *was* worth it, it *was*. At the same time, he is trying to leave. The contradiction is tearing him apart.

This young man has also reacted with fury to an excerpt from Virginia Woolf's *A Room of One's Own*. In the same hour, we covered an essay, also by Woolf, called "The Mark on the Wall," that had upset him just as much. The essay follows Woolf's thoughts as they meander around the subject of an unidentified spot on the wall she sees from her chair. She can, she acknowledges immediately, get up and see what it is. But this would be to take the easy way out, to do too much honor to the way the world is usually presented and described. For in our usual scale of values, a mark on the wall is lowly indeed and certainly not worth worrying about. Yet, she suggests, this hierarchy of values is only a convenience that excludes far more than it includes, and should not be confused with reality itself.

For example, it would demote to the status of a mere preparatory state the condition of not knowing what the spot is.

And are such states of ignorance regarding the world not the rule rather than the exception? We should beware of proclaiming them not meaningful. Moreover, getting up to find out what the spot is, and so in some sense reestablishing mastery over it, would be to keep up the notion that we control the world. Is this not another of our fond illusions? Woolf lists objects we lose, then points out our ignorance of the provenance or final end of the things that seem so solid to us. How much more chaos than order there is in our contact with the world, how much more uncertainty than certainty! Far better to acknowledge the sea of ignorance in which hard facts swim.

It takes, I suggested to the students that day in class, an act of courage to give in to uncertainty and acknowledge it, as Woolf does in this essay, rather than doing the thing she had been told so often by others to do: put an end to it, deny it, just get up and see what the spot is. Such acknowledgment of disorder may give a more accurate portrayal of the world. Woolf's illustration of the illusory nature of this order is the "Table of Precedency" from Whittaker's Almanac: who sits next to whom among the ecclesiastic and aristocratic ranks, who precedes whom in a formal procession, who enters the dining room first and who last. By the 1920s, she tells us, people had largely ceased to believe in this table, and the whole had begun to seem like a ranking of the angels in heaven, and of as much use. No order is permanent, she implies; all is construction. She understands the point of such construction (what she calls "nature" trying to preserve its creatures), but does not for that reason accept the invariable claims of those who do the constructing, namely that this order is something they found, rather than created.

Woolf shows us, I suggested to the students, that our love of order and hierarchy blinds us to everything in the world that doesn't fit into the ordering, namely disorder and slack moments. Think of drill, I tell them, the parades on Wednesday afternoons. The order tourists so love and the military commanders strive to produce is nothing but a fact of perception, not to mention preparation and artifice. There's no order in a parade from the point of view of an ant—which in fact is why so many of Woolf's pieces are written from the points of view of small, insignificant creatures, the seminal short story "Kew Gardens" for one. In this story, if that's what it is, fragments of conversation between different groups of people walking in a garden are intercut with a "drama" of a snail trying to get over a leaf. Swift's Gulliver, when shrunk to the size of a thumb in the land of the giants, finds repulsive the gaping pores in the skin of even those women held to be the most beautiful of the giantesses. An audience member straying into the middle of one of Annapolis's marching companies would suddenly lose the sense of order that is so evident to those perched where they are meant to be, up in the stands. And then the parade is over. They march off to a place where the audience can't see them let out their breaths, unbutton their stifling jackets, and relax.

What makes us human is neither the achievement of order, which thrives on exclusion, simplification, and ignorance, nor the worship of weakness and outsiders, but instead the impossible striving after an order we can, by definition, never absolutely and for all time achieve. Keats knew this, and said it in his "Ode on a Grecian Urn." I want to tell them what Sartre knew, namely that we can willingly and temporarily loan our freedom to a structure to give ourselves a definition in the world, but we cannot ever escape that freedom. The burden of being human is that we must strive for awareness. We can never escape the responsibility to choose.

I would say, however, in contrast to Sartre, that the desire to escape this responsibility is also part of what makes us human: the dream of having someone else determine our selves is a powerful one for us frail creatures. Sartre saw only what he called "bad faith," a kind of fundamental lie, and the worst there is. Precisely because, in Sartre's terms, we are always Becoming and never Being, it is precisely Being for which we long. But the siren song of Being, that is to say, absolute certainty where we know all answers before the questions are asked, must be resisted, for it lures us to our own deaths.

Acknowledgment of the disorder sacrificed either consciously (as in drill) or unconsciously (as in the fact that we simply are not aware of all we overlook, the slack moments of our minds' wanderings, those that Woolf is putting on paper for us to see) is what Woolf asks of us. She wants us to acknowledge our low moments, acknowledge those times when it seems that the world has spun off its axis. The Naval Academy by contrast tells us: grin and hide these times from others, suck it up, put on a happy face, do not dwell on failure. Success is all that counts. Woolf says: failure is the norm. If we choose to strive against it, it must at least be with the knowledge of the power of what we wish to overcome.

Woolf's essay, I acknowledge as we discuss it, is non-motivational. Nonetheless, and precisely for that reason, they should have read it. But no, I admit, it may not be what we should tell the grunts. And it wouldn't encourage anyone to storm San Juan Hill.

Later that same day I find myself speaking again of storming San Juan Hill, this time to my plebes. For the memoirs of Robert McNamara have just come out, co-authored by a member of our history department. I was attempting to link McNamara's *mea culpa* regarding a war he now feels to have been unjust, but to which he sent thousands of Americans, to Wilfred Owen's condemnation, in his poem "Dulce et Decorum Est," of those who tell "children ardent for some desperate glory" the "old lie, dulce et decorum est / pro patria mori."

I told them that McNamara's acknowledgment that the war was wrong should pose problems for them. I suggested that they think about it. What if this were 1968 instead of 1995, the streets outside the Academy filled with protesters agitating against the thing they were being trained to do? Certainly they would be busy defending their superiors. Now, decades after the fact, their superiors admit that they were wrong. What if their superiors admit, thirty years from now, that they were wrong about whatever it is that the students are now so busy defending them against? Should this possibility affect their actions now? Think how futile it will all seem, I tell them, as futile and destructive for all concerned as the Vietnam conflict. I am now having the conversation I avoided with Tim O'Brien's "The Things They Carried." Some days I'm up for it, some days I'm not.

Circling the Wagons

THE CONVICTION THAT the worst was over for the Academy when we had weathered our cheating scandals turned out to be false. Who could have predicted the breadth and sheer variety of our subsequent problems, or their oddly differing degrees of relevance for us as an institution? Surely the 1994 suicide of the Chief of Naval Operations, not a graduate of Annapolis, is peripheral to the Academy, even if it is central to the Navy: purportedly the reason was unearned medals. The debate rages over whether he was entitled to wear a "V" for valor on several of his ribbons; could this have been an honest misunderstanding? I am uninterested in the technicalities: I see the man at the helm of the Navy deserting it. How can he be forgiven for something for which a sailor would not be forgiven?

Then, in short order in the mid-1990s, there were such oddities, right here in the Yard, as midshipmen being arrested for such actions as child molestation (most of my students thought this was all the worse because both the midshipman and the child were male), car theft, and, more threatening to us as an institution, drug use. How to react? One option would be to adhere to the pretensions of the institution to absolute integrity and claim that the miscreants were a few bad apples: this is, unsurprisingly, the administration's stand. Or should we see, as much of the press and not a few outsiders have seen, a pattern of moral turpitude that is deep-seated in the very fabric of things here in Annapolis?

In the 1995 Naval Academy sesquicentennial, workmen attached flags to the streetlights in the Yard. I saw them being put up one morning when I arrived to work on syllabi for the upcoming semester. The flags were blue and gold, the Navy's colors. 150 YEARS, they read, the same sort of vertical banners held between two staves that have become ubiquitous in the "theme" downtowns of refurbished American cities, or that give cute names to parking sections at suburban malls. In Annapolis, where the mall advertises itself with the sign of a sailboat, the flags sport the names of Chesapeake Bay wildfowl: heron, duck, and egret. The decorative flags here at USNA were some PR person's notion of a good idea, cousins to the "country" banners that hang from the houses around my brick duplex, stitched with mushrooms, horses, autumn leaves, even a few wreaths and Christmas leftovers.

One afternoon during the first week of classes in this kick-off of the sesquicentennial year, we faculty members sit in the newest building in the Yard, Alumni Hall, to hear the new superintendent give his first "State of the Academy" address. This building began life as the "Brigade Activities Center." The cornerstone, laid the first year I was at the Academy, preserves this original name at least in its initial letters, the BAC. Then they realized they could begin to ask the alumni for money, and they changed the name.

I cherish the memory of the construction of this building. That spring, the English department had agreed that every professor and officer would teach, as well as novels chosen individually by each, a single common one: Faulkner's *As I Lay Dying*. The spring was hot, and because of an aging air-conditioning system (the building wouldn't be renovated for another fifteen years), I opened the windows. Next door, at the BAC, they were driving piles, as the over-sweet, too-heavy air poured into the classroom and blurred our students' brains, already addled by Faulkner's purple prose, endless sentences, and looping chronology. For a second, then two, then three, there would be silence. Then would come a heart-stopping "WHUMP" that we felt in the floor beneath us as the machine came down on the pilings. Then once again one, two three, "WHUMP," and over, and over, and over, like the madness-inducing reiteration of a dripping faucet in a prisoner's cell magnified to the point at which it rocked the world, a reiterated, completely predictable earthquake. I'm not sure how much they got from Faulkner that spring.

Within Alumni Hall almost a decade later, that sesquicentennial year, the Admiral reports, in what seems relief, to his utterly silent audience of civilian and military faculty members rising in tiers before him, that press accounts of the Academy have begun to "turn around" after the rash of scandals, with positive stories now appearing once again, especially in local papers back in the hometowns of midshipmen. A good part of what we do at the Academy is about how we are perceived: just as the perception that an officer—or a politician—is in control helps that person stay in control, so the perception that the Naval Academy is an upright, A-OK place is its own reward.

This admiral has come to us from the Sixth Fleet, after having already been superintendent. The year he himself graduated from the Naval Academy, back in the late 1950s, he was Brigade Commander. Obviously our overseers think he will whip us back into shape. Now, he tells us pleasantly, he commands not the Sixth Fleet but only the 300-plus acres of the Yard. We are meant, I think, to feel his descent in the world. Or that with a more restricted field to work on, his command will be that much more focused and intense.

We hear that Congress came closer this time, after all our scandals, to considering shutting us down or turning us into a one-year postgraduate school. Sending this admiral was the alternative. He has to get results.

He tells us that, in the past, we at Annapolis have made the mistake of trying to compete with civilian institutions by becoming more civilian. In fact, we should be doing what we do best, namely, being military. We are, he tells us, "held to a higher standard." Higher, that is, than the civilian. I sometimes suggest to them that there is a contradiction that they have pledged to put their lives on the line to defend such scum. Yet at the same time, I reflect that to a certain degree, belief in the greater purity of life here inside our walls seems necessary to compensate our students for its rigors. If they are not better than the world out-side, what is it all for?

Some of what the Admiral has to say this afternoon is what he clearly thinks the troops need to hear, about having turned a corner, about his being available, about everyone working to-gether. He concludes his remarks by taking questions. There are few. We all stand up in unison as the Admiral leaves the podium, and then we disband.

The Admiral has listed some things he noticed were on the increase when he returned to the Academy. One was "cynicism"; another was "individuality." These, we gather from his subse-quent remarks, are to be discouraged. Again and again we have heard the phrase "core values." I wonder what they would think over at St. John's of "individuality" somehow making it to the short list of sins. Or rather, I know.

We must build character, the Admiral tells us. Implicit in this statement is the assumption that we know what character we should build, and that we are well on our way to figuring out how to accomplish this, as if character were like a superior ship's hull. As strongly as these assumptions are being questioned in some circles, they are just as strongly being reasserted at An-napolis, turning a corner out of what is increasingly labeled, the better to distance us from ourselves, a "period of laxness."

The students I have talked to are bitter about the draconian measures taken as a result of what before were minor (and in-deed, in a less hysterical and siegelike atmosphere, may well still be minor) offenses. Their cynicism is not diminished by their perception that they are being made the fall guys in a conflict that has nothing to do with them, or that the rules are applied selectively. On one hand encouraged to push the limits (Nietz-schean T-shirt of a skinhead Marine officer in the gym: THAT WHICH DOES NOT KILL ME WILL MAKE ME STRONGER), they are punished swiftly and sharply if things can be perceived to have gotten out of hand.

One of the new rules that has been put into effect as a result of our ongoing scandals is that midshipmen must wear uniforms when outside the Academy on all but a very few occasions. I found out about this when a group of my students came to my house for dinner. The doorbell rang, and my daughter Alexandra, then about six, and I went to open it: I expected a group of blue-jean- and leather-jacket-clad short-hairs; instead I found a cluster of uniformed midshipmen who, when asked, spilled their resentment at not being able to socialize in civilian clothes. The rationale for this change of rule is that midshipmen are supposed to be proud of their uniforms. "Yeah," says one student, holding a plate with a slice of chocolate cake on it at dessert time. "If we wear them more we'll be prouder of them. Just like chocolate cake. If you like one slice, you'll love having the whole cake crammed down your throat." He mimes gorging and then choking.

The day after our "State of the Academy" address, I pick up a copy of the "USNA Strategic Plan (Second Update)" that is lying in unread piles in our mail room. So peppered are we with strategic plans, with Total Quality Leadership, with Zero-Based Overhauls of this and that, even the faculty can hardly help being guilty of precisely that cynicism the Admiral found to have increased on his arrival back here in Annapolis. Part of this problem is the fact that each admiral promulgates his own

Strategic Plan; of course it seems to him to be the answer to all problems. The fact that we civilian professors stay around and suffer through three or four of these in a decade is not something that occurs to him. Nor is our input solicited in any but a pro-forma fashion, if at all; we are expected to fall in line and show "loyalty."

The cover of the particular Strategic Plan I picked up after the Admiral's sesquicentennial welcome is one of those graduation-day photographs that makes the heart of every military man swell in pride. For once it is not the hat toss. This one shows a row of resolute young men (and one young woman) with right hands raised, taking the oath that makes them officers in the U.S. Navy. The photograph has been carefully chosen and cropped to include the woman and a dark-skinned male. All are clean-cut, all are gleaming. All look determined: foes of the U.S. beware.

Inside, I read of goals for the Naval Academy. Under "vision": "Our graduates are imbued with the highest ideals of character, leadership, professionalism, and service." "We are a TEAM." "We value the cultural and ethnic diversity of our men and women." Under "Guiding Principles," I find "Teamwork": "We are committed to the principles of teamwork, selfless service, professionalism, mutual respect, trust, free and open communications, concern for the well-being of the individual, and an appreciation for cultural and gender diversity." Can all these principles be served simultaneously, I wonder? Can rationality and order ever triumph over their opposites? Can people be convinced to do right? Can two fundamentally opposing points of view ever be made one through mediation? The recourse of the human race to war on repeated occasions—the reason, after all, for the existence of institutions such as the U.S. Naval Academy—gives us serious reason to doubt that this is so. And gender diversity? This at so-male Annapolis, where the urinals were left in the women's heads (toilets) for a quarter-century after women were admitted? They merely changed the sign on the door: for me this was a metaphor of the way we "accepted" the arrival of women. Perhaps people thought the women's inclusion was just a passing phase. I should know, perhaps, that these pamphlets are window dressing for journalists, or for Congress, and not meant to be taken seriously by those in the know.

The Admiral Defends
Academic Freedom

SOME OF THESE questions about our so-beautiful-sounding PR claims resurface in an op-ed piece published in *The Washington Post* later during our sesquicentennial year by a temporary member of our faculty. He was an ex-Marine (as most people would say; Marines say, "Once a Marine, Always a Marine") who had sold real estate, was initially hired as a hockey coach, and was kept on in various capacities afterward at the behest of the football-player superintendent who presided over the cheating scandal.

I opened the paper one Sunday morning to find, on the front page of the Outlook section, an article by this James M. Barry, whom I had never heard of but who was identified as "teaching at the Naval Academy" in our department of Leadership and Law. Entitled "Adrift in Annapolis," it came complete with a large drawing of a Gilbert-and-Sullivan-type admiral going down in a foundering rowboat labeled "U.S. Naval Academy." Always up for a good tussle, my initial reaction was to think: What fun!

I was both amused and disappointed. The article, I found, started well and ended badly. It hinted at a possible link between the disastrous 1991 Tailhook convention, recently in the headlines at that point and so useful as a journalistic "hook," and the Naval Academy's scandals. The article's subtitle, written of course by someone at the paper, was: "To Understand Why the Navy's Moral Compass Is Broken, Start at the Naval Academy." According to the article, our students ("these wonderful young people"—already I could tell that this was going to be a praise-the-troops-and-damn-the-officers article) "become immersed in an ethically corrupting system."

Barry went on to describe the system as "so powerful that, by the start of their second year, most of [the midshipmen] are confirmed cynics who routinely violate regulations about clothing, driving, alcohol and sex, plus any other rules they consider superfluous." What else is new? I thought. Much was made of diary entries by students expressing frustration and distrust, apparently culled from submissions to the author's own classes. Several paragraphs were devoted to charges that women are routinely harassed, and the middle of the article was spiced up with the report of a rather odd case in which the relationship of a female officer with a male student was allegedly continuing.

Recommendations of remedies followed. I smiled and nodded when I read that "we should de-emphasize varsity sports," but furrowed my brow when I got to the assertion that "we should eliminate tenure and institute three-year contracts for civilian professors." Many allegations, however, hit their targets. Barry was clearly right, for instance, in his perception that our students come here starry-eyed and quickly become disabused of their idealism. I'd add that because the hierarchy is so clear-cut here, the chances for abuses of power, as for the necessity to cover up insufficiencies, are infinitely greater than in the real world. And since the search for truth, based on open, frank debate, does in fact take a distinctly subordinate position to "loyalty," the chances of getting things resolved based on rationality alone are slim.

I smiled in agreement as well at one rhetorical question in the article's closing string of several: "Can we let go of the zero-defects/looking-good mind-set long enough to face reality?" Or, it went on, "will we continue to shoot the bearer of bad tidings?"

If this final question was a trap, our Admiral leapt into it with both feet. Which one to do? Shoot the messenger, of course! The article appeared on a Sunday. By Monday, Barry had been removed from the classroom. An "all-hands brief" was called for the faculty in the BAC—or rather, as it was called by that point, Alumni Hall, in honor of its collective donors, its corridors perfumed for me with the heavy scent of Faulkner's magnolias. Since going to the Admiral's first "State of the Academy" address at the start of our sesquicentennial, I had vowed to no more be a part of this overly respectful audience. (Attendance at such functions for civilians is only "encouraged," not mandatory.) Instead of joining the stream of people going to hear what he had to say, therefore, I headed for my car and home.

It turns out I missed a hell of a show. With the by now much-maligned author of the article sitting in the audience, the Admiral, according to all those who were there, grew red in the face, pounded the podium, screamed that he had been "betrayed" by this man whom he did not deign to name. Barry himself sat in stony silence; the faculty listened and said nothing. How glad I was that I hadn't been there—though of course, at the same time, how disappointed. Would I have been able to get up and leave to protest the ranting of this madman, threading my way up the aisles, all eyes on my back? Or would I, as is more likely, have sat in the same bitter confusion as my colleagues?

The Admiral had his say that afternoon. Yet others apparently realized that this was not the military at its finest. In fact, the lawyer of the Navy's top officer, the Chief of Naval Operations, we heard, berated our Admiral for such a personal attack, and the civilian-run *Navy Times* ran an editorial roundly condemning his actions as an example of how *not* to exemplify the slogan he had coined on arrival, "Excellence Without Arrogance." For a while this appeared over the lintel in our bookstore and in countless other places. A personal attack on a faculty member showed, in the opinion of the *Navy Times* editors, just such arrogance as was supposed to be discouraged. In the opinion of the faculty too.

By Wednesday, the American Association of University Professors had intervened, and Barry was back in the classroom, to the unconvincing strains of administration explanations that he had been removed "to work on a report." The Admiral made an admission that was undoubtedly meant to be disarming: he had been "thinking like a C.O." rather than like a college president. He had, presumably, for the entirety of his first three years as superintendent, before my time, never been shown to be misguided in thinking of himself as a C.O. and not as a college president. Was it all those people sitting in silence and rising when he turned to leave the first time around that made him think he was on the right track?

In his article, Barry had offered a list of cynical "Rules of the Road" he claimed had been compiled by midshipmen. One was: "Loyalty is more important than truth." That's pretty basic, I thought. For that matter, the Admiral himself bore this one out in spades. For what enraged him the most and made him red in the face that day at his meeting was, apparently, his perception of having been, in his words, "betrayed." In the Admiral's view, this professor should have come to him with any complaints he had about the way things were being run so that he, the Admiral, could consider them and have the last word; the outside world would never know the complaints had been made. This, after all, was what he was used to from his years as Admiral of the Sixth Fleet. In the military, as in the Medieval feudal system, relationships of inferior to superior are personal, and abstract truth cuts little mustard. Embarrassing or even questioning your superior in public is the big no-no. This may be true in business too (thinking like a CEO), but what makes colleges and universities different from any of these institutions is precisely that the pursuit of Truth is supposed to be beyond individuals. If you can prove your point, you prove your point, no matter what your superior thinks of it.

The military obsession with loyalty, like those of its political and business-world counterparts, stems from its need to guarantee precisely what humans do not usually offer: predictability. How else can you be sure that the many individuals who are necessary to fight a battle will in fact act in concert? Machines can be constructed to be predictable, but human beings are more iffy. If they can be made to prize loyalty, however, you can breathe easier—assuming you're the one they're loyal to. Loyalty, as Nietzsche would have pointed out in a heartbeat, is a virtue only from the point of view of those with the upper hand. Underlings can at most ask for protection: they cannot ask for "loyalty" from a superior. An officer is concerned for his troops, he is not "loyal" to them. What relevance has a specific, almost technical virtue like this to an institution of higher education? We professors are first and foremost loyal to the abstract concept of Truth, or should be if we are worth our salt. Individuals come later, if they enter into it at all. It's the opposite of the way the military sees things.

The conflict ended up epitomizing the tension inherent in teaching the humanities in the context of a military setting. Though he was a civilian professor taking on an admiral, in a kind of twist-about, Barry ended up showing himself as a member in good standing of that group of our critics, usually hardline military men such as former Secretary of the Navy James Webb, who have argued that USNA has become too academic.

Barry, Webb, and those who agree with them hold that, instead of teaching subject matters, we should be teaching "leadership." Everyone knows that leadership is charisma, and hence is something we are born with. Or if it is made, it is made individually, as a result of quirky sets of circumstances that force a single person to the forefront. How can it be produced en masse? Yet in the current hype we are a "leadership laboratory," a nicely alliterative phrase I have never understood: are we producing leadership? Testing it? Are the scientists of the implied analogy the leaders, or those who are making them?

Despite the obvious degree of personal enmity between the professor and the Superintendent, both men seemed to agree that standards at the Academy had become lax. At issue was merely whether the problems predated or had continued into the current administration, which at the time of the article had been in power only a year and a half. Understandably, with the Admiral's reputation on the line, he would have found this particular issue of dating a central one. To many of the rest of us, it seemed beside the point.

Barry, the Admiral who felt so betrayed by him, and critics such as these show themselves as brothers under the skin: all those involved in the battle were clearly nostalgic for the Good Old Days, a kind of Eden where students toed the line and things worked as they should. Barry's article suggested a time roughly contemporary with his own arrival at the Academy, some seven or eight years before, as the Good Old Days' last gasp; the Admiral in some pronouncements talked more in terms of fifteen years. The Spartans, represented by critics such as Webb, went a decade or so further back.

But why stop even there? Surely in their heart of hearts they all know that the Good Old Days ended in 1955, or was it 1958, when the Admiral graduated as head of his class? At any rate, a time before Vietnam had tarnished the public's attitude toward the military, a time before majors were instituted at USNA to break up the unified curriculum and before a library was built, a time when the press preserved a hands-off policy of apparent ignorance of the hazing and racism that marked the Academy in this Eden—and perhaps not coincidentally, before women were admitted at all, or any students other than middle-class whites in any appreciable percentage.

The odd implication behind the Admiral's push to remilitarize, which he announced on his arrival, is that students who act like their counterparts in civilian universities by wearing shorts, or by addressing their classmates normally, have a propensity to become child molesters, thieves, or cheaters—the odd ball-up of disparate scandals that had preceded his arrival. Civilianizing equals immorality. "We need to do what we do best," said the Admiral. More is more. He tightened the rules. As a result, it became an infraction for students in the first two years even to own civilian clothes, much less to wear them, or for students to call each other by their first names, save if they are of the same class and in their rooms in Mother B.

This tightening of standards was, we were told, requested by the students themselves. The Academy is merely giving our students what they want. But in point of non-trivial fact, those requesting the new tightening were not the student body at large but the stripers, the Brigade leaders. Stripers are those of the students sufficiently in sync with the military system to have been chosen to assume roles of military leadership as students. Besides, all of the Eastern European "people's democracies" justified their repression on the grounds of popular demand, measured (or invented) as the leaders saw fit. In a pinch, you can say you know what the people really want, even if they appear to be saying the opposite.

Piling Sand

SOMETIMES IT SEEMS as if there is no rationale at all for the rules handed down and enforced so summarily. At a recent faculty meeting, we were addressed by the Commandant, the Navy captain in charge of midshipmen's military education, whose place in the hierarchy is equal to that of the academic dean, just below the superintendent. I was amused by his body language: older man addressing the troops, hands on hips, jaunty strut despite his pot belly, his skin sagging from too much sun and, we hear, too much liquor. Because he is not directly involved with us, we feel more willing to ask him embarrassing questions, as we instinctively avoid doing with the Admiral, or the academic dean who must sign off on our pay increases.

A colleague of mine in the English department raises her hand.

"Have you ever done studies on the effects of sleep deprivation?" she asks. "I've been doing some reading about recent experiments with eighteen-year-olds, who need longer sleep, especially in the morning."

The Commandant is speechless, though trying to be affable with this room full of people he does not understand, civilian PhDs. "Well," he begins, then stops.

The colleague tries to help out. "I mean," she explains, "we see them sleeping in our classes and dragged out, unable to concentrate. Maybe you just need to be letting them sleep more. It would certainly make our lives easier."

When I first came to the Naval Academy, I sat in this very science lecture hall and heard a Navy captain, now of course long gone (this again is the fundamental fact about the Navy personnel; they have hardly arrived before they leave), go into the various strategies to discourage sleeping. These ranged from throwing chalk (makes an impressive mark on their dark uniforms) or erasers (an even more impressive one) to banging the table or shooting them with water pistols. I have done none of these things, preferring to keep track of who is doing what and address the next question to anyone whose eyelids begin to droop. In cases of general fatigue, say on those days when they have gotten up at 0430 to jump out of helicopters or when more than a few of them have been awoken in the middle of the night to take a "whiz quiz," to pee in a cup for drug testing, I simply stop the class for a mandatory "stretch break" or lead some motivational push-ups between the desks. Still, I think the point is well taken: I myself am unable to digest anything of any depth when I have gotten fewer than my usual eight-and-a-half to nine hours sleep; when I go to bed after midnight I feel the effects for days, and I have taken an afternoon nap (twenty minutes, start to finish: makes me a new man) since I was sixteen.

"Uh, no," says our affable commandant, momentarily ceasing his comfortable addressing-the-troops pacing back and forth. "We've never done any studies. Don't know anything about that."

The presupposition must be that constant sleep deprivation for four years can prepare one for, and somehow make one more effective under, fleet conditions. But has this presupposition, that people can "get better" at functioning in a sleep-deprived state, ever been tested? Has it ever even been articulated? Even if it is true, does radically reduced functioning for four years of intellectual development justify whatever slight improvement in functioning ability later on it might carry with it? Should we torture the midshipmen daily to "prepare" them for possible eventual torture as prisoners of war? ROTC students put on a uniform once a week, make their beds any way they like, if at all, go out into their college towns, and still join the Navy, the Army, or the Air Force. Are we to assume they cannot distinguish between what is appropriate behavior generally and what is appropriate behavior when in uniform?

The MIT linguist Steven Pinker, in *The Language Instinct*, cites the case of an African tribe that believe they must pile sand around their babies to help them learn to sit up. The proof that this is necessary is that since time immemorial, the parents have piled sand around their babies—and the babies have learned to sit! You don't want to be the first parent with a child who can't sit as a result of going out on a limb and trying to do without this method.

Much of what we do at the Naval Academy seems to me to fall into the category of piling sand around babies. The claim is that future officers need this kind of group-think, this humiliation, this constant policing, the constant stream of demerits, in order to be effective leaders. But I've never heard this corroborated by flag officers. The skipper of the Aegis cruiser we went on—the one who told us to give the midshipmen hell—said that he saw no difference, after a year or so, between the ROTC officers and the USNA ones. Indeed, he noted, himself a USNA graduate, that the USNA officers had an exaggerated view of their own importance that stood in the way of their being effective with the enlisted men and women.

Suddenly, before this so-affable commandant who didn't even understand what issue was being raised, it seemed horrifyingly possible to me that in fact there was no justification for this vast machine so carefully oiled and tended except the circular one of its own self-preservation.

III

Don't Slam Me

DURING THE SUMMER after their second year, the students go on cruise. So, one year, did I. A submarine cruise. I discover, not for the first time, that the idea of being a servant of a great machine is strange to me.

DON'T SLAM ME, reads a sign on the door to the head in the Los Angeles–class nuclear submarine on which I am a two-day visitor, I'M IN THE SILENT SERVICE. A stylized dolphin swims between the admonitory lines, the same symbol of the submariner that disports itself in symmetrical pairs on the chests of many of the officers and crew. Sometimes on surface trips, the men tell me, dolphins will play off the submarine's bow. I have seen this on ships.

Not only the doors to the head carry this warning not to slam, but the doors between sections of the corridors as well.

Only the huge watertight door to the engine room, behind which lie the complicated intestines of the nuclear reactor and its attendant machines laid out like organized tan-painted spaghetti, a door which must be cranked open, is without this label. Its watertightness is a safety measure: if the functional part of the ship, from which protrudes the screw that moves it through the water, floods, the watertight door will ensure that at least the remainder of the crew outside this section is saved.

Sound carries. This is what we may not forget. It carries especially well underwater, and through solids. Any noise within the ship, its skipper tells the group of us "VIP" visitors around the wardroom table the first night, carries through the shell and can be read as human noise by an enemy ship's sonar, betraying our presence. Anything that is not the clicks and pops of normal life underwater can betray us: doors slamming, a wrench dropped into the bilge. The idea is to lurk, unknown, black-painted on the outside and full of light and machines, within the light-starved depths of alien waters. Noise kills. Silence is all.

Until only a few years ago, the submarine service truly was the "Silent Service." Very little was divulged to the outside world about these soundless-as-possible cigar-shaped killing machines, whose success in the 1970s and 1980s was measured primarily in terms of what they prevented from happening. Merely knowing that such potential launching pads of warheads were off their coasts is supposed to have deterred regional tyrants as well as the Evil Empire from carrying out their worst plans. The threat was multiplied through secrecy: the more of our submarines that could be imagined to be suspended in the depths, the greater the deterrence. Silence not only within the ships, but concerning them.

Silence aboard the submarine is still enjoined, but silence concerning the submarine fleet has been abandoned. That first night in the wardroom and on several occasions thereafter, we visitors find out why. We find out at the same time why we are being treated so well. For there is no question but that our position is privileged: we are allowed in practically all nooks and crannies, the men are polite to us as we clog the corridors, and time has been set aside for the officers to give us tours. We are even allowed to drive the ship, one of us sitting at the wheel that tilts the ship's nose up or down, another controlling the lateral movements.

As we find out, the secret to steering well is not overreacting. Used to automobiles, with their instant and visible reactions, we all swing the wheel wildly to left or right, feeling no reaction and thinking we have failed to turn enough. The rapid sinking or rising of the red digital numbers on the control panel before us, after a pause of five or six seconds, sends us careening wildly in the opposite direction. Pushing in on the depth wheel makes the ship dive; pulling up makes it rise. We gradually learn to dampen our enthusiasm, and in any case the great dark ship reacts only sluggishly to our adolescent-style joyriding and stays, more or less, its course.

The skipper, a businesslike graduate of the Academy, is by his own admission more comfortable with actions than with words, and he seems glad to leave the talking to the admiral who is getting in his sea time by accompanying us. This admiral, also a USNA alumnus, is in charge of the entire group of submarines of which this one is a part. He is almost stupefyingly articulate, and very clear in explaining the reasons for things—such as the fact that if he does not go on a submarine two days a month, he ceases to draw his supplemental sea pay. Or the fact that we have been invited on board in a conscious effort to publicize the submarine fleet, something that only a handful of years ago would have been thought highly dangerous and unnecessary to boot.

In the deep freeze (or hot frenzy) of the Cold War, the necessity and desirability of the submarine force was taken for granted. Money was flowing. Military hardware was a desirable commodity. Nowadays, the justification for such amazing microcosmic worlds as the one within which we sit, many hundreds of feet beneath the Atlantic on our way from the ship's home base of Groton, Connecticut, to Annapolis, is less self-evident. Hence this almost crushing assault of human charm. The Admiral reiterates that, though the Russian submarine force sits largely undeployed, it still contains submarines at the peak of technical excellence. Which, in the world of submarines, means submarines that are fully as quiet as, if not quieter than, the wondrous machine around us. We are engaged in a costly war of silence—a new submarine runs between 1.5 and 2.5 billion dollars.

Silence has now given way to volubility, night to day, secrecy (within limits) to disclosure. The aim of the submarine service, watchful silence, is a curiously voyeuristic aim, I think that evening, as I survey the world of virtual reality spread out in the blinking numbers, glowing bar graphs, and complex grids on the screens of the control room, existing in what is at best a highly mediated relation with reality. What subs are meant to do is watch, and wait. But it is through mechanical eyes that they watch, and what they see are numbers and charts.

In front of us are machines that, in case of offensive action, will be programmed by software to fire off torpedoes or missiles at ships or land targets. The operator will not even know what the target is when he puts in the disc. There are screens that show large and small maps with updated information on the position of battleships. On other panels are the numbers that tell us where we are in the ocean: on the surface, or within the range where we must begin to fear for the pressure of the water upon our hull. In an adjoining room, men stare at the sonar equipment, where dandruff-like snow is the norm and on which experienced eyes try to read patterns in the static that might be other vessels. Here the world is translated into its mechanical equivalents, with which living human beings must somehow interact. Success in battle is translated into two glowing blips intersecting each other on a silent screen; disaster could be measured in a column of rapidly dropping numbers, the liquid-crystal display flickering with the bony joints of right-angled numbers itself oblivious to the implications of the death it is telegraphing to those within the ship.

Of course, there is the periscope, whose data, if still mediated, comes a bit closer to "reality": when the ship rises to the surface of the water, the operator can actually look at images from the world, though themselves reflected back and forth on mirrors. And, with the permission of the Chief of the Watch, we visitors can mount in the "sail" while the sub is on the surface, go up the ladder to that graceful spine-like protuberance on top of the submarine that breaks the water first. Up here on top, there is room for several men, if they sit on the side, each harnessed to a cleat. A passing wave drenches me, and I come down.

We visitors, with a couple of extra visiting officers, are put in the nine-man berthing, whose roominess ranks somewhere between the staterooms of the junior officers (only the captain and the executive officer have private rooms), each of which contains two beds, and those rooms meant for the men, each of which contains twenty to thirty beds. I have been assigned to a bottom bunk, and must slide in by holding on to the edge of the top bunk in the stack. The man in the top sleeps under boxes and controls only inches from his nose; for me it is the reading light and the bottom of the shelf above my head that would give me a nasty bruise if I were to toss and turn in my sleep. Coffin-like though this space is, it is nonetheless the only place on the ship that gives me anything approaching privacy. With the curtain drawn up the side, I can at least read here, or lose myself in meditation, or nap to offset the effects of the unaccustomed schedule. These include the fact that, underwater, the days are eighteen hours long, divided into three six-hour shifts; meals are served four times a day, and only the fact that the earliest one includes eggs and bacon indicates (if what I am told is right) that on the surface it is morning.

Aside from my bunk and the head, where the user hesitates to linger, there is no privacy. The officers' wardroom, which is our public space for the time we are on board, is usually either being used for meals (two seatings at each mealtime, save breakfast, as on a train) or is full of people talking. The lack of space means that physical proximity is unavoidable. The corridors are so narrow that people must brush by one another; in the officers' head, two of us are lined up in our towels by the single aluminum sink waiting for the shower stall, with a third man having to edge by us to shave at the sink.

Looking for space, I have seized upon mention of the "exercise room." I ask if I may see it, naïvely imagining something like the cramped but adequate room with a few Universal Gym machines I used on board the cruiser several years before. The reaction to my request is considerably more hesitant than I have been programmed to expect in this world where I find myself the honored guest. I must be escorted, it having been determined that I do in fact have the necessary (minimal) security clearance to penetrate into the sub's innards, where it is located. I persist, or rather simply wait, and soon a seaman arrives to accompany us. He is smiling; for him this may be the alternative to more onerous duties.

We go through the airtight door into the engine room, making our way through turbines, air scrubbers, reduction gears, and the equipment to make fresh water. Suddenly the seaman stops and tugs at a tarpaulin under one of the tan tubes between which we have been making our way. "This is the rowing machine," he says, and sure enough, in a moment the tarp reveals the fins of a machine tucked in under the curve of the giant tank. "You have to pull it out to use it," he explains. This is a model with only virtual oars, or rather a mechanism that does not protrude. "You put it back when you're done with it," he adds, somewhat unnecessarily.

There are, in addition, an exercise bike—which even when repositioned requires the rider to lean sideways and crick his neck while riding it—and a cross-country-ski machine tucked away in another crevice. The long space between turbines in which we stand is wide enough to do push-ups in, he explains. It is also the smoking area.

"Smoking area?" I ask, aghast at thinking of the self-enclosed atmosphere on board. Our guide explains that smoking will soon be prohibited; until then it is permitted only at several fifteen-minute intervals during the day. Later I am in the engine room again during a smoking interval; the alarms go off and we must leave the area, which the lieutenant who accompanies me told me is always what happens at smoking time. Though all know the alarms are the result of the cigarettes, the threat is treated as a real one.

On this first visit to the engine room, my interest has deflated quickly. I am disappointed to find that the "exercise room" is in fact only a few pieces of equipment shoved under machinery, and I realize that I had imagined a refuge from the reality of this so-compacted world. The seaman confesses that few of the men have what it takes to keep up fitness over the long haul, and the machines are infrequently used. On the way out he runs his hand across a ventilator grid and shows us the oil film on it. "The air is full of oil," he tells us. "We're breathing it right now." He looks at us, then away.

In fact there is no private space, no recreation, no respite from the machinery that wraps around us and that I and my fellow visitors alone are exempt from serving. I have visions of Fritz Lang's 1927 fantasy film *Metropolis,* in which proletariat workers whose bodies have been all but sacrificed to a vast network of subterranean machines toil to ensure the leisure of those who play on the surface. The men here live and breathe (quite literally, according to the seaman) the machinery, sometimes for six months at a time, at what must seem the whims of the government, or the development of foreign threats. The following day I recognize a former student, a lieutenant, who tells me that he had one day's notice last fall before having to bid goodbye to his wife of less than a year. The ship returned six months later. Still, that's the kind of duty he'd signed on for.

Not all the time was spent underwater, of course, though the point of nuclear power is to permit virtually unlimited submersion. As the skipper proudly tells us several times in the course of our journey, only the amount of food the ship can carry caps its ability to stay submerged. A submarine makes its own fresh water, cleans its own air, and discharges its waste: this was some of the machinery I saw.

Exceptionally, during this trip up the coast all waste is being stowed so as to comply with the stringent Chesapeake Bay requirements. The result is the bags of trash we see in the pantry the next day that must be taken out to get at the canned food. How much food can it carry? we ask the supply officer escorting us. Three months' worth is considered the normal maximum; four months is stretching it. In the case of a period exceeding ninety days, food must be stored under bunks, in crevices (battened down, of course, so that it does not shift in case of tilts), and in seats. Already it fills the benches in the crew's mess, is piled on enclosed shelves, and generally seeps between more substantial shapes.

The ship carries a crew of about a hundred and thirty men. Where do they all sleep? I wonder, having seen only a few of the dormitory-like cabins. I find out on a visit to the torpedo room, at the front of the ship. Under the suspended torpedoes is a space of a few feet between the underbelly of the weapons and the floor of the ship. On this shallow shelf, at the level of our feet, are arranged what seems a wall-to-wall sea of mattresses, laid out in two rows. Mattress touches mattress, separated only by flimsy metal dividers at the end meant for the men's heads (which face in, meeting in the middle of the two rows of length-to-length bedding that can be fit in under these hanging cartridges). On my first visit the mattresses are empty. Later, when I come by again, I see rows of hairy legs and feet protruding from under the missiles: men trying to sleep during their shift's programmed "night." We visitors are not encouraged to be particularly quiet, and the chief petty officer, or "chief," in charge of the torpedoes is voluble in his enthusiasm. On the way out, I ask how the men can sleep in all this light and noise. The question itself seems to surprise him. "They get used to it," he tells us dismissively.

Sleep under the torpedoes, the all-but-naked bodies of exhausted, celibate men laid out row by row underneath the great hanging genitalia of this ship, multiple phalli whose expulsion is the reason for all the complex machines around them: if this is not sacrifice to the great Moloch of the machine, I have never seen it; it seems to be a total dedication of human lives to hardware. At present, of course, no women are permitted in the submarine service. I have seen how complicated it would be to fence off areas of privacy, even how difficult it would be to find the space for two sets of toilets. And I can see why openly gay men would pose a problem.

The men who sleep inches from the torpedo casings probably have gotten used to it. The question I pose about whether
men were meant to sleep under the weapons like this, as cans of
tuna fish are stowed under bunks or the rowing machine under a
turbine, clearly seems odd to the chief in charge of the torpedo
room. I insist, rephrasing: "Surely the sub can't have been designed to have men sleep here."

Suddenly he understands how strange this must appear from
my landsman's perspective. No, he agrees. The sub is not designed this way. These sleeping arrangements are in fact more
humane than the intended alternative, namely having men sleep
in shifts in the more permanent groupings of bunks, in a practice known as "hot-racking": the rack, or bed, is imagined not
even to cool between the men who sleep in shifts. This utilization of otherwise wasted space under the hanging torpedoes
that seems so inhuman to the outsider is actually a step toward
giving each man his own private, albeit small, place.

The Chief is exultant, dancing back and forth from foot to
foot like a prizefighter. "This is what it's all about," he tells us. "It
kills them that they only exist to serve my torpedoes." He runs
his hand lovingly over the casing beside us, underneath which
protrude several pairs of naked feet. He explains the capabilities
of his weapons, explains that the casing drops off the torpedo as
it exits, projected at a slight angle to avoid the sonar equipment.
The torpedo ostensibly containing nuclear weapons is a mock-
up only, he tells us, and pats the container. They use it for practice.

Missiles are intended for land targets: the advantage of
shooting them from a submarine is that they are launched from

international waters, and from secrecy. No U.S. land troops are threatened. The Chief makes much of the way these are targeted at specific buildings miles away on dry land, and of their accuracy. I do not mention the way the touted accuracy of these missiles claimed, in the early days of the first Gulf War, to be near 100 percent, has since dropped alarmingly.

The intended target of torpedoes is other ships. The torpedoes are wire-guided, I learn to my surprise. Each trails an umbilical cord that lies coiled up at its base and unravels as it travels. This wire allows fine-tuned steering; when it breaks, the torpedo can still guide itself, albeit not so well as through the wire, directed from the ship. To me, knowing nothing of how these weapons work, the wire seems almost charmingly atavistic, quaintly old-fashioned. That such hardware would, after all, still have to be attached in some way to the mother ship seems to me proof that the principles of birth hold good even here. Only when they explode is the cord ruptured.

The way the torpedoes work is not by penetration, as we might expect given their physical appearance, but by creating a giant air bubble when they explode near the hull of the enemy vessel. The air bubble the missile creates raises the target ship out of the water and then creates a hole in which the enemy vessel, while splatting back down into the water, twists, or breaks its back.

Utilization of all space, dedication to the mechanical whale that surrounds us and through whose entrails we make our way: this is the nature of life on a submarine, a life made possible only through the cultivating of meticulous, sober action by all men at all times. That first night, as our discussion in the wardroom grows more metaphysical, the college president along on the trip—the president of St. John's College, as this ship is the U.S.S. *Annapolis*—asks how the nature of warfare from a submarine can be made to jibe with traditional "military" virtues of strength and courage. He is referring, I think, to the passivity that has become a virtue here, and to the meticulous reading of data that replaces the swinging of a sword.

The skipper seems not to understand the question. This is merely his life, the job he was trained to do. I am struck by the way the exultant Chief in the torpedo room stroking his gleaming casings contrasts through his more traditional warriorlike enthusiasm with the ranks of screens and blips on monitors of the control room. The Chief's bearing is the exception in the ship as a whole. For those in the control room, is serving this war machine like manning any other machine? Or do they too think themselves warriors? By the time I leave the ship, I still do not know.

The last day, when we surface to make our way up the Chesapeake Bay—treacherous ground for all boaters, I am told—there is an all-hands reveille at 0445. Shifts are disregarded; all the men are up. After the public-address system goes silent, I manage to sleep again. When I stumble out of our berthing around 0700, I find the corridors aglow with artificial daylight and the men going busily to and fro. The artificial night is equally startling: the evening before, I had to make my way in utter darkness along the corridor to the control room, crashing into several dark shapes of men along the way and muttering apologies, only to find the control room itself plunged into near-equal darkness broken only by the flickering of the screens.

Twelve hours later, the navigator, a young lieutenant who graduated from the Academy the year I arrived, is still charting the ship's course, relaying each direction to the Chief of the Deck, who relays it to the actual ship's driver. The Executive Officer is dragging but alert. The Skipper has been up in the sail since the wee hours, talking on his walkie-talkie and watching the landmarks that the man at the periscope is reporting down in the control room.

How do they do it? I wonder. My eyes had begun to blur after a few minutes. These young men have their specialty, I have been told: the driver always drives, the radar man always watches the radar. There is not even the respite of variety. How can this young man watch the numbers rise and fall for six hours? Not to mention six months times six hours?

Giddiness can be fatal, and daydreaming is discouraged. There is no room for levity, despite the long hours. The day before, the navigator has talked us through our course up the Chesapeake, mentioning each buoy and lighthouse as if we would remember them. He notes that there will be a tendency to high spirits, with port and four days' liberty approaching. "You have to catch that early," he notes soberly.

Seeing such businesslike dedication to duty, I am almost glad to have caught one of the screen-watchers fooling around with a computer program showing what ships are where in the Mediterranean. I ask what he is doing; the Executive Officer is tolerant. "He's just bored," he says. In a minute the young man, scrawny and a bit pockmarked, rises from his seat to draw a half-inch-long addition in felt-tipped pen to the chart of the ship's course splayed out across the wall. Then he sits down, and a moment later is once again, at least in his own mind, off the coast of Greece.

This part of the journey is at periscope depth. The night before, we surfaced, and all the visitors were invited into this very control room that now hums with efficiency and relayed commands, manned by tired-looking men swigging the eternal coffee from cups set in wire no-tip baskets attached to the edges of tables and to poles. In one of the public-relations videos we were shown the previous afternoon (spookily self-referential, I thought as I watched the produced-for-the-public rah-rah videos about the necessity for submarines while I sat in the wardroom of one, like the tiny replica of the house in Edward Albee's *Tiny Alice* that catches fire when the house around it does), we have watched a submarine make a spectacular surfacing maneuver, surging up to the surface like a nose-up whale, spewing white foam and arching down to horizontal on the surface of the water. Since this, an emergency surface, is a technique that the crew has to practice periodically to make sure they can do it, the skipper decides to give us a treat. We will come up off Norfolk with flair.

We stand, scarcely daring to breathe, in the pitch-black control room, where red numbers provide no help to eyes unused to the darkness, in a space that in darkness bears no relation to the room we have by now seen so often in the light. I have to be led to my position, and I'm planted on a chair. Even so, I step on a man's leg and feel dark shapes all around me.

The square numbers on the control panel flicker and our depth increases. We go down to four hundred feet. The depth is relayed back and forth in the darkness. The captain gives the command for an emergency surface. Suddenly we feel the room tilting. I hold on to my chair. The numbers flicker by. Three hundred. Two hundred. When they flicker past fifty, then forty feet, we abruptly feel the world heave above the surface and fall back. It is a gentler feeling than the video would have suggested, a graceful rising rather than a surge. Now we are on the surface, where we will remain until we dock in Annapolis.

This also means we are once again subject to the ebbing and swelling of the waves, and I go to sleep that night with a prayer of thanks that I am not subject to seasickness. The next day, once again on dry land, I spend several hours feeling the fluids in my ears sloshing back and forth. Or so it seems, my body having unconsciously internalized the motions of the ship in an effort to convince itself that they were normal and flatness the abnormality.

To the seaman who showed us the rowing machine and who told us that with each breath we inhaled oil, I said, perhaps somewhat fatuously, "I wonder if God meant people to live under the surface of the sea." He replied: "I wonder the same thing. I have three months before I get out of the Navy."

Friendship

ON THIS TRIP, I have seen a former student doing his job: proof that I have been here at the Academy for a non-negligible period of time. And when I return to my office to prepare for the upcoming semester, I pass another milestone of this sort. The office next to mine bears a nameplate that looks familiar. Randy, from my favorite group of honors English students, is returning to teach plebes for a three-year tour after five years as a copilot on F-14s. At the time, the waiting list for pilots was prohibitively long and he wanted to take the earliest available position. I wonder what it will be like to have a former student as a colleague.

The situation turns out to be not without problems. One day, I am parking by the building and see a little red car zip up and into a space nearby. Out steps Randy, five years older than when I saw him last, stockier and fuller of face. Is this, I wonder briefly, the young man who sat with his tennis shoes up on the edge of my table and wrote agonized prose on the subject of "The American in Europe"? Who one day at my house talked about brotherhood and jockstraps? Part of me is annoyed: here I spent countless hours with this guy, and he doesn't even so much as drop me a line to let me know he is returning.

Randy sees me, smiles, but hangs back. Clearly he is not sure what the protocol is. I decide to break the ice.

"Come here, you lunk," I say to him, and when he is close enough I ignore his outstretched hand and give him a pounding hug on the back. He reciprocates somewhat tentatively. We unclinch and shake.

"Why the hell didn't you *tell* me you were coming back?" I say to him mock-indignantly.

"Well," he says. "Yeah [this in acknowledgment that I have a right to be annoyed]. Hi." The smile is forced.

Suddenly I realize he doesn't know what to call me. "Hi, *Bruce,*" I correct him.

This gets a real smile. "Hi, Bruce," he repeats, and pumps my hand.

"So what have you been up to?" I ask.

"Flying missions over Iraq," he says.

"Bombing all those innocent civilians," I say.

"Hell, yes," he says, grinning. "The more the better."

We still understand each other. I feel encouraged.

I go back to Topic A. "You still haven't told my why I had to learn from looking at your goddam *door* that you were coming back," I insist.

Even if I'm "Bruce," I am still the professor, and I can demand accountability.

This is the moment of truth. Randy is silent a moment, looking down, then up. "Well," he says, "maybe I wasn't so sure how you'd feel about seeing me again."

"Oh, for God's sake," I say, pretending to find this ridiculous.

"I mean," he offers, "I gave you hell."

I understand this as the apology it is. "You sure did," I tell him.

He smiles and relaxes. The conversation grows general. What about me? he asks. A lot of water has gone under the bridge with me, I tell him: I am no longer married to the woman he saw me so in love with. I have a daughter. Things change. Finally he excuses himself and, after another handshake and a "Bye, Bruce," at which he laughs, still finding it hard to call me by my first name, heads off in the opposite direction. We'll end up spending a lot of time together, this fall, most of it in the weight room.

In the Weight Room

WE HUMANS, AS Sartre and the phenomenologists pointed out, are most fundamentally the rush of our flow through the world: Existence precedes Essence. We *are,* before we are anything in particular—liquid wine before bottles that contain it. As a result, we suffer from the constant desire to taste ourselves as solid creatures: we strive after solidity. To a certain degree, we can attain this visually. If we are alone, the mirror gives us some sense of ourselves as seen from the outside. The gaze of another can make us solid. We can find solidity in sex, taste the boundaries of our being as solidified by another.

For me, this leads to the weight room, which has given me a real understanding of the universal male need to be bested. Another man is simply competition, a creature too like ourselves to give us what we seek. Where to turn? To the quivering sensation of being unable to lift an iron-laden bar even once more. In that moment, I meet my match. It's a sensation for which I think many men yearn, though most of us will not accept it at the hands of another human being.

In Hitchcock's *Vertigo,* the black-gloved Kim Novak, whose role calls for her to play at being a woman inhabited by the spirit of her long-dead ancestress, poses absurdly in her haute-couture gown at the slice of a giant sequoia preserved in Muir Woods, north of San Francisco. She points at one of the rings in the huge, centuries-old tree trunk. "Here I was born," she says melodramatically . . . she pauses: "And here died." Here, I can say, putting the pin in a stack of weights, I begin, and here end.

In the weight room we come to feel both the point and the inadequacy of Wittgenstein's drawing in the *Tractatus Logico-Philosophicus* 5.6331: under a teardrop-shaped balloon seemingly inflated outward by the smaller circle identified as the eye, the philosopher remarks: "The visual field does not have this form." The philosopher's point is that we are our perceptual worlds: the visual field is not in the world, any more than death (in a later proposition) is a part of life. We are inside the balloon, and so cannot conceptualize it as a balloon from without.

In college I thought this was profound. Now I think it's merely inadequate. This is a philosophy written by someone who, with all due respect to the tortured genius that was Ludwig Wittgenstein, *did not pump iron.* In fact, our relationship with the world is more active. Had he gone to the weight bench, his arms trembling to move the bar to a final repetition, his spotter grunting encouragement from behind and protecting his chest from being crushed, he might well have realized that in fact, so far as our physical world goes, we have some control over the balloon. We taste the limits of our bodily power in our own muscle failure. It is failure, but it is at least our own failure, and it is self-induced: something we have sought and, ever so briefly, tasted—from within. In the weight room, failure is our goal. We seek to define that point in the world where our power fails: in that point we taste the limits of our being—not from without, but from within. Success is only the necessary but uninteresting means to what we are really seeking: self-induced abnegation, tasting limits that we can, ever so slowly, force to expand.

We like the hardness of the weights, the clank of the plates and the solidity of the bar. And the fact that every time, some number of plates is guaranteed to get the better of us. That's the point where we sense the living membrane we constantly push outward between ourselves and the world.

Randy and I read the muscle magazines, trying to find new ideas. At the end of a workout we can hardly stand.

In between lifts and grunts, we talk. Randy tells me what it was like to take my courses. He won't get mushy to my face, but it is clear that he and I hit it off, even then. "You didn't try to cut somebody's balls off," he tells me in approbation one day after preacher-bench curls have left us quivering. "It's not your style. You give them a hit and then show them how to try it again."

"Um," I grunt in acknowledgment.

He tells me why he came to the Naval Academy. He turned down a sports scholarship to Yale, afraid that he would turn into a no-good frat boy with no direction. "I was afraid of the freedom," he offers. "I guess I thought I'd feel secure at Annapolis."

"And did you?" I ask.

"For a while," he says.

Many of our students, I think, feel secure. At least for a while.

Randy is coming to terms with the strange sensation of being on the other side of the desk in the classroom, and he runs by me his experiences with the plebes. I make suggestions. One day, he asks me to come to his class in order to react. What I see is a supremely confident, infinitely likable young officer who has the eighteen-year-olds eating out of the palm of his hand, hero-worshipping him like crazy. I grin. At the same time, there are two or three holdouts, the principal reason he has asked me to come. I think once again about the overwhelming role charisma plays here at USNA, how the person giving the information trumps the information itself.

It is fun watching him charge ahead, and watching the students eagerly follow. His one or two problem cases are simply silverbacks in training, young male gorillas thinking of challenging the lead male for the predominant position. I tell him to squash them relentlessly; they'll love him for it afterward. "Drown 'em in testosterone," I tell him.

I feel as proud of him as if I had been his father the day he explains via e-mail to one of his recalcitrant plebes the meaning of duty and self-sacrifice—he's sent me a copy to let me know what's going on. It's all about how one observation by the senior officer is supposed to send the junior officer (or in this case, the plebe) scurrying to find ways, on his own initiative, of making the officer's expressed wish reality. And the senior is *never* supposed to have to remind the junior of rank. If he has to, the junior has already failed.

Yes!, I think, reading this. This *is* what the Navy is supposed to be about. My chest swells to the point where I can feel my heart thumping. Still, this obsessive will to please another man, all-consuming though I know it can be and perhaps necessary though it is in the attenuated climate of the military, is not my thing. I much prefer to look on from the outside. I think of the doctor in Pierre Boulle's novel *The Bridge over the River Kwai*. In the well-regarded film by David Lean, the doctor functions as the Greek chorus: he wears a uniform too, but his job is to patch up the men who get hurt. His valedictory to the testosterone fight between the British officer and the Japanese that is the ironic paradox of both book and movie (the POW British officer builds the Japanese a better bridge than they would normally have gotten in order to make his equally captive men proud of their work, even though it is for the wrong side) is this: "Madness! Madness!" My valedictory might be the less dramatic one of "Yes, but—"

The most bonding time I spend with Randy consists of grunts and body language. But I read some of his writing and note to my surprise that he writes far better now than he did five years earlier. I mention this one day as we are stretching on the floor. "What happened?" I ask. "What's different now?"

He laughs. "The fact that now I have some real responsibility," he says. "You realize when you graduate that the buck stops with you." Then he laughed again. "That, and getting enough sleep," he added. So much, I think, for our "leadership laboratory."

The gym has allowed us to transform the student/teacher relationship into one approaching that of younger brother/older brother. I know that Randy won't always need this relationship, at least not in this form, but he does now. I need it now too, in the wake of my disastrous marriage. Randy's return has been a great gift to me. He embodies my own history. He was a student during my first year here; now he hauls ass with me over to the gym, sometimes in the cold and rain. He likes me; I like him.

Most of all, perhaps, I like his enthusiasm. Randy has more energy than ten ordinary men. He believes that he has served his country by coming to Annapolis. It is important for him to know that he has, at least for a period of his life, placed himself in harm's way. But he can still joke about it. "Tip of the spear, my friend," he says, grinning broadly. "Tip of the spear."

Most of my students simply disappear. Randy didn't. He's like the few children of Charlotte the spider, in *Charlotte's Web*, who returned to the barn door the next year. Somehow it makes things seem all worthwhile.

Yet nothing is forever. Time passes. Randy stays a bit longer, then leaves in his turn, getting out of the Navy, going to business school. He finally parts ways with his wife, who has always remained a somewhat shadowy figure and about whom we rarely talked. For the first time, I hear about how unhappy she made him.

We talk occasionally on the phone. In the gym, I had pounded him with stories of my unhappy first marriage. He took them in without much reaction; there it was appropriate for his response to be merely a grunt.

Now he has stories in his turn. Why only now? I ask.

For the longest time, he tells me, he wouldn't even allow himself to realize that he was unhappy. When finally his wife refused to join him in his new job, it was as if he'd been given a "get out of jail free" card. He'd never have had what it took to break it off.

"But, Randy," I say over the phone (by now he is in Seattle), "could you have lived with the pain?"

He laughs ruefully. "That's what the Naval Academy taught me," he says. "How to live with pain."

Displeasing the Administration

IN FEBRUARY OF 2003, I was on sabbatical for the second time since I began to teach at the Naval Academy. And one evening, almost at the end of the month, getting on toward the anniversary of Keith's death eleven years before, I was reminded with a slap of something I had simply chosen to forget since the Barry affair: how badly a military structure tolerates dissent. As a soldier's own complex emotive life disappears behind the question of whether he will or will not pull the trigger at the right time, so all the things that make me me—my books, my quest to get students to think for themselves—disappear behind the all-important question, Am I predictable to the administration?

My wife Meg and I were reading in bed, close to turning out the light. The phone rang. She answered it and handed it over to me.

It was the Academic Dean. He had called to "encourage" me to withdraw an article of mine, upcoming that weekend in *The Washington Post*, on the Supreme Court case deciding whether the University of Michigan law school could continue to use race as a major deciding factor in admissions. I had e-mailed it that day to my department chairman as a courtesy. Through the magic of computer technology, it was in the corridors of power within minutes.

The Superintendent was noted for bullying and demeaning people around him, including this very Academic Dean and everyone unfortunate enough to be around him. This style of "leadership" had apparently been found good enough for "Top Gun," the school at Monterey made famous by the movie all our students have seen many times, the Superintendent's previous command. The Dean was responsible for keeping the faculty in line. Clearly he hadn't, at least not in my case.

Meg's analysis later was that this was not a request that the Dean had seriously expected to be granted, but only a call that he thought his superior, the apparently short-on-patience Admiral, would expect him to have made. This way he could say that he had called me and asked me to withdraw the article, and that I had refused. Ire would fall elsewhere than on his head.

The superintendents of all the military academies had, only weeks before, issued a communal denunciation of the suit against Michigan. My superior had spoken; my job was simply to shut up and say, if asked (of course I wouldn't be), "Sir, yes, sir." Going out of my way to agree publicly with something my superior had already pronounced on would have been presumptuous and redundant. Exponentially, almost unthinkably worse than that, I was publicly expressing a contrary opinion.

The Dean acknowledged my right to write such a piece, he assured me, and to publish it. He was asking, he reiterated—not ordering—that I withdraw it. He had defended me previously, he said, when I had written things about the Naval Academy, but it would be difficult to defend me now. To me that sounded like a threat, not a prediction.

Then he went on. It would not be good for me, he said, or for the English department, or for the "whole sabbatical system" if this piece appeared. Furthermore, there was no way he could explain it to the Admiral, our Superintendent, who was hopping mad. He knew I would understand.

I didn't. "What exactly am I being threatened with?" I asked.

There was a moment's pause.

"Nothing," he assured me. "Nothing."

Nor could he, would he, specify what sort of deleterious effects on the English department, my own career, or the "sabbatical system" he might have had in mind.

There was silence, the phone weighing more heavily on my chest, my wife listening at my side. "Well," I said to gain time, "I hardly know what to say."

This noncommittal answer on my part somehow seemed to break the back of the conversation. It went on for some minutes but ended with the Dean telling me that this was more a "personal call than a professional one," as if he was mollified by the mere fact of having said his piece.

"You're a big boy," he said. "Gird your loins."

Gird my loins? Gird my *loins*? Tenured professors are supposed to publish. Was I supposed to feel grateful that I was not, as the hapless Dr. Barry had initially been, to be ripped from the classroom? Was this only because, being on sabbatical, I wasn't in the classroom this year to begin with? Did the American Association of University Professors have to intervene *again*, to explain yet again the meaning of academic freedom and the tenure system to which the Naval Academy purportedly subscribed? The Barry incident had been before this dean's time, though he had heard about it, he had said when I had pointedly reminded him a few minutes earlier.

I lay there beside Meg, who was by now breathing peacefully in sleep. I by contrast was rigid and awake. I repeatedly assure friends who ask me what it's like to teach at the Naval Academy that it's like anywhere else, except that the students wear uniforms. What a fool I'd been. Another fulminating admiral used to getting his own way and with no experience with the exchange of opinions that constitutes liberal education had come on board—and a new one did come on board, with clockwork regularity, every three years—and everything began again from zero, all the lessons had to be retaught, as with the plebes every fall.

Affirmative Action

MY DISAGREEMENT WITH the assembled brass—and agreement with the Bush Administration—came from having spent an increasingly uncomfortable time the year before as a member of the Academy's admissions board. Every Wednesday night we read applications. We spent every Thursday around a long table either giving or hearing briefs on applicants before voting whether they were "academically qualified" or not. This wasn't admitting them: voting that they were qualified was only one step in a complicated journey to Annapolis that could be derailed at many points, though voting that they weren't qualified meant they weren't coming.

Rather than allow someone whom the Dean of Admissions wanted admitted to be voted down, however, there was the option of assigning the applicant to a category to be admitted applying lower standards. Prospects for this group included candidates desirable because of their race, their ability to fill a place on an athletic team, or their already being in the Navy or Marine Corps. Much to my surprise, I learned that only half the class actually has to achieve the standards we hold out as our minima.

Race was the subject of the Michigan case. I am probably more fearless talking about race in public than is usual for a white American, by dint of having lived in Rwanda, where everyone (outside a handful of foreigners), from the president down to the lepers that worked on construction, was, by American standards, black. When I went jogging down the rutted roads of volcanic rock near the small humanities campus of the university where I taught, in the foothills of the Mountains of the Moon, the small boys who ran delightedly to the road to cry *"Mzungu! Mzungu!"* (Swahili for "white person") left no room for doubt that they had noted, and were commenting on, my skin color. Africans in Francophone Africa speak about *les blancs,* white people, and *les noirs,* and are utterly unapologetic at noting the skin color that in America is supposed to have become invisible.

As a result, I take badly to our euphemistic American labels that try to fob off a color designation as if it were a nationality, and that seem to suggest that everybody is some sort of American, the only problem being to determine what kind. A few years ago, one of my students, trying to speak about the characters of Chinua Achebe's now-classic *Things Fall Apart,* which is set among the Igbo in precolonial Nigeria, referred to them as "African-American." I corrected him, then laughed, realizing that for him, this was merely the polite way of referring to people with dark skins and what we call Negroid facial features (some southern Indians, Dravidians, are as dark as most Africans). The African-American Igbo of what later became Nigeria: what a hoot. And the thing is, my student thought he was just being delicate. What, in our terminology, is an African-Haitian? An Arab-African-American? An African-Caribbean-Quebecker? A white South African-American? Nowadays, we love our labels. I don't. "African-American" is an absurd overcorrection, an attempt at euphemistic gentility that muddies the waters.

Living in Africa has also made me very impatient with the white = slaveholder, black = slave assumptions of American politics—or their somewhat diluted correlate: white = oppressor, black = oppressed. In Africa, all oppression prior to the white colonization in the last few centuries was black on black. The Rwandan civil war was black on black. It was the black Africans who organized the slaves to be sold to the Europeans.

Nor can we blame Christians in particular. In America, there's a tendency to believe that Islam is a more Africa-friendly religion than Christianity. In fact, Islam was exported to Africa by force by white Arabs. Arabs have held black slaves for centuries. Slavery, largely of black Africans, was legally abolished in Arab (white) Mauritania only in the 1970s, and according to many observers it continues de facto to this day.

From my year on the admissions board, I learned that the Naval Academy practices a form of affirmative action, based on race, that makes sense at all only when expressed in abstract terms, not in the particulars of individual cases.

It's difficult to be without sympathy for the intended out-come of such preferences. It does seem important to have black and Hispanic officers when many of the people in the fleet are black and Hispanic. That's why the military brass had supported Michigan in the case. It's not that a black Marine needs a black officer to inspire him to follow orders, only that he or she needs to know there are such, somewhere, maybe even right here. A lot in the military depends on "morale," that difficult-to-quantify measure of people's satisfaction. Sometimes we have to do what we say. It wouldn't be enough to say that of course Miss America could be black, if she never had been.

The difficulties arise when you start asking how to define the groups to which you're going to give preferential treatment. Be-fore students come to our board, the computer generates a num-ber (called the "whole-person multiple") that takes into account their grades, their rank in class, their test scores, and their ath-letic and extracurricular activities. Being a child of an alumnus adds a bit to this score, but only as much as, say, an especially good essay, or of having done well at our Naval Academy sum-mer seminars for high school students. In any case, each of these adds only a small amount—500 points—to the total score: 68,000 is considered a solid admitting score, and 75,000 is stellar.

Members of three racial groups receive preference at USNA: African-Americans, Hispanics, and Native Americans—at least this was true the year I was on the board. I've since heard that suddenly we have "enough" Hispanics, and they're not on the list of protected minorities any more; I don't know whether or not this is true. The Academy practiced and so far as I know continues to practice a "two-track" admissions policy with the racial minorities to which it wants to give preference, precisely what the Supreme Court said Michigan could not do. Racial-minority applicants have their own minority members of the admissions staff, who present them on a separate "track" to the board, clearly marked as minorities. The implications for a student being presented in this fashion as being a member of one of these three protected minorities are immense: there is quite a gulf between the two tracks.

First of all, in practice we drop the figure for minimum SAT scores by about fifty points for each test, for a combined total of a hundred points. If a "majority" student scores 600 in the math section and 600 in the verbal section of the SAT I, we put a check mark next to the name and go on to other things. If a "minority" student gets in the neighborhood of 550, we are generally satisfied. For a "motivated" minority student in the low-500 range, we generally recommend a remedial year at the Naval Academy Preparatory School, if this is consistent with other things in his/her record.

A year taking remedial courses at taxpayer expense was presented to us as "seeing if the student had what it took for the Academy," but in practice all a student has to do to go from NAPS to the Academy is achieve a C average (2.0) in their remedial courses. And students with lower averages are regularly granted exemptions from this requirement. All but a few students who attend NAPS do subsequently attend the Academy. They take precedence over that year's more qualified candidates, who compete for the remaining slots. The idea isn't to scrape off the cream, it's to get all these minorities to Annapolis. One year, a Hispanic applicant sued the Naval Academy on the grounds that he had been turned down because of his low test scores. The fact is that in practice we already require lower scores from Hispanics than from white or Asian students. His were even lower than these.

The most spectacular effect of being briefed to the board as a member of a racial minority is that if we don't send him or her to NAPS, the student is directly admitted, if voted in by the board and managing to pass the rigorous physical exams. (Effectively, NAPSters are admitted directly, only a year behind.) Such a student doesn't have to stand in line and be ranked for one of the nominations coming from congressional or executive sources that otherwise is the sine qua non of admission. A "majority" student may be voted academically qualified by the board and pass his or her physical exams. At that point the student becomes one of up to ten students to whom a Congressperson can give a nomination for a single slot. Of these ten people, it's possible that nine will ultimately be sent a letter saying "no." (They can get in from someone else's list, or by being a set-aside of another sort.)

Sometimes the Congressperson lets the Academy choose who gets the nod. In these cases, it's the person with the highest whole-person multiple who gets in. If the Congressperson wants, however, he or she can designate which applicant gets the nod. And an overwhelming proportion of the students to whom the institution offers admission accepts their offer of admission.

Of the up to nine students per Congressperson who do not get in, all may well have had multiples higher than that of the minority student who was admitted directly and who was not only held to lower standards, but did not have to compete further. These rejections are what give the Academy its reputation for being a hard-to-get-into school. I've heard so many stories that I can't count them anymore about stellar high school students with athletic prowess losing out on this essentially chance lottery—and I've heard just as many adults tell me, when they hear I teach at Annapolis, that they tried to get in and didn't. People never forget.

Who are the beneficiaries of this amazing admissions advantage? That was what caused us problems on the board. Membership in such categories at the Academy is established based on self-identification. At least, that was the final directive during a year when it seemed that a good deal was being made up as we went along. Early in the year, we were told that when a student checked the box saying that s/he "identified" as Native American, we could ask for confirmation of tribal affiliation. (The student may check as many boxes as s/he wishes; if one box is for one of the three "protected" minorities, the student counts for our purposes as among this group.) Yet by mid-year we were being told that we could not legally ask for confirmation of tribal affiliation, or of "Hispanicness" or "African-Americanness." If a prospective student identified him- or herself as being, perhaps among other categories, of one of these groups, the applicant was to be considered as such.

This led to apparent howlers like the student with a Scottish last name attending the flossiest private school in central Texas self-identifying as Hispanic and so receiving preferential treatment. Early in the year, one applicant told an admissions officer she was one-eighth Hispanic: this was enough, and in any case we subsequently learned we couldn't even question the label.

What was the point of all this inequity? we asked. Initially, we were told that the Department of Defense was seeking to have officers who "looked like" the sailors and Marines, who are disproportionately African-American and Hispanic. Fine, I said, let's ask what skin color the applicants have. I suggested, in my best Swiftian mode, that we send out paint cards with varying skin tones and ask applicants to circle the one closest to their own: browner than a certain level would lead to preference, lighter would preclude it. I hope the irony of the suggestion was understood, but the reaction I got was (of course) horror. We can't do that!

Someone whose parents emigrated from India, who can be very dark, is not a protected minority in this sense; someone whose parents arrived from Ghana is. Hispanics, of course, can have any skin color from white to black. I have had students with Spanish (European) parents who entered Annapolis with preferential treatment as "Hispanics." Many Cuban and Dominican Republican immigrants are by most people's standards (as well as their own) white. We had discussions on the board: does someone from Brazil count as Hispanic? They speak Portuguese, and so are Lusophone. Someone from neighboring Ecuador would be Hispanic, by contrast.

Were we doing this to rectify past injustices? Why should the child of Ghanaian immigrants who had never suffered from slavery be classified as "African-American"? Why should a rich kid with a grandmother from Puerto Rico be given preference as

Hispanic? To such questions there were no answers—because there can be none. Grouping people always results in inequities in the gray areas, in individual cases. That's why there are always objections to it.

The largest single group of set-asides, about 17 percent, is, however, not based on race at all. It's got a more immediate purpose: the staffing of the Academy's athletic teams. Many of the students in this group are also sent to NAPS, where they get a year older and stronger.

Of course, the Naval Academy isn't the only school where playing a sport gives you a leg up. In recent years, books by Manny Sperber (*Beer and Circuses*) and Derek Bok (*The Game of Life*) have explored the obvious facts that athletics gets many mediocre students into top-flight schools, and that athletes represent a huge proportion of the class (teams don't get smaller if the school does) at selective liberal-arts colleges. For every one of these athletes who sits in a classroom chair, there's one fewer much more promising student in the room.

It's bad enough, for me anyway, to think that people get into Yale and Williams because the baseball coach needs a shortstop. But it's simply unacceptable at the Naval Academy. We "hire all our graduates," as a superintendent who held office in the early 1990s liked to say. They not only are supposed to graduate—athletic recruits at State U. don't put graduation high on their list of priorities—they *have* to graduate to serve as officers in the Navy and Marine Corps. And that means they're responsible for big decisions that involve expensive technology and, very possibly, people's lives. We shouldn't be choosing our future officers because we want a winning basketball team.

Ignoring athletic prowess, or at least not making it the tail that wags the dog, may seem like a quaint suggestion, which would make college teams like sandlot baseball: we make a team out of whoever shows up. That's not the way things work at other colleges nowadays. The subtitle of Sperber's book is "How Big-time College Sports Is Crippling Undergraduate Education." Undergraduate education is the only kind we do. This would be a terrific chance for the Academy to actually live up to its pretensions to being better than the rest of the world. If we could get the other academies to agree, we could compete only with them, if we liked. But I bet we wouldn't have to. We'd probably have a pretty good team—any team—if we waited to see who showed up. Our applicants are almost universally athletic. That's the kind of kid we attract, the football captains and the lacrosse players and the runners and the swimmers. They get points for that in their whole-person multiple. Lots of points. In giving preference to the ones we usher in the front door "direct," we take sometimes-large academic hits to get the All-State Whatever. The issue isn't encouraging physicality—a given at our institution; certainly the "happy in my own skin" demeanor that athletes typically have is a benefit in command. But everybody here competes, or practically everybody, and everybody has to pass the PRT.

Athletic recruiting is about staffing the teams, not the well-being of the Navy and the Marine Corps. Once the athletes are in, moreover, they're in: someone recruited for a position on a particular team isn't separated if he or she decides to drop the sport because it takes too much time, interferes with academics, or causes an injury. So their added value is gone, the taxpayer is footing the bill, and they're taking up a seat for which somebody better qualified was turned down.

Sometimes the argument is made that victorious sports teams keep the alumni, who give money, happy. That's been shown at most institutions (see Bok) to yield internal money, funneled to the sports teams themselves. In any case, Annapolis is government-funded. Alumni money comes in handy for add-ons, but it's not necessary for our day-to-day running of the institution. Finally, the kind of student who would have heard of Navy merely because its football team was victorious isn't necessarily the kind of student we want.

The last group of set-asides, more than 20 percent of our class, is the fleet admissions, students who typically flubbed high school and joined the Marines, or who come from the Navy, most typically the nuclear program. These are almost all sent to NAPS. In theory, we're rewarding them for being the top Marine in their group, or the #1 Nuclear School graduate. In reality, it's not just the #1 Marine we let in from the fleet but, in some feeder pools, virtually all the applicants. I've heard from several of my "priors" that admission to the Naval Academy is used as a recruiting tool for the Nuclear Power Program. They're told up front that the majority of those who apply from this program are offered admission to the Naval Academy, either directly or through NAPS. Many of them spend a year or less in their respective services. They can't have been in too long, or they're too old for the Academy; twenty-two is the maximum entering age.

The Hollywood version of these fleet admissions postulates hardworking sailors and Marines pulling themselves up by their own bootstraps, a view that made more sense in the 1940s, when

Annapolis was virtually the only way up and out. We get some golden ones. But the average is pretty average. They too take up seats.

The admissions staff likes to say we're "taking a chance" on these invariably nice young men and women, all our set-asides. But what about all the others the board voted "academically qualified" who never made it to Annapolis? I know that when I voted "academically qualified," I thought I was saying this student was more worthy of being at the Academy than someone I agreed had serious deficiencies and so needed a year at NAPS. For me, the big surprise—and the one I'm still shocked by when I consider its implications—is that the student with the serious deficiencies is virtually guaranteed a slot in next year's class. The superior student we voted into a "higher" category of "academically qualified" will in all likelihood fail to make it to Annapolis. He or she may have the misfortune to be applying from a competitive state, or fail to win the slate of a Congressperson who designates the "principal," the one student who gets the nod. Even #2 on a slate filled using the whole-person multiple is likely to be very good, and he or she will be offered admission only if it can be from another slate, or for another reason.

Chickens Home to Roost

THE SLOW STUDENTS determine the speed at which I can advance in the classroom. That's usually not very fast. Sometimes the speed slows to a crawl. Everybody loses out. Before my stint on the admissions board, I accepted this as the way things were: we couldn't get students any better than I had. Now I knew we could, and that we turned them away.

At the six-week marking period of the semester after my sabbatical, I turned in a record number of the reports we have to turn in periodically on students earning Ds and Fs. (Students are not permitted to fail entire courses without breaking through many safety nets.) I couldn't fathom it. There just weren't supposed to be this many in February, I thought, not after a semester of this stuff under their belts. And the failing students were very weak indeed; they couldn't make subject agree with verb, they couldn't make an argument.

The classes seemed worse too: day after day going over the same material, midshipmen not getting the point. Was I simply in danger of burning out? Had I been spoiled by my sabbatical? It took serving on the admissions board, something most professors never do, to make me realize that half our class was let in the back door, under less competitive circumstances and typically with lower indices of capability than those we usually use as our minima. And that these students are taking the places of the brighter ones.

I pulled up the records of my D and F students on the computer, newly savvy to the meaning of the shorthand I saw, and the implications of having come to us from NAPS, and what it meant if they said they'd been recruited to play for a team—and for that matter, knowing now that this was relevant information. With one exception, every weak performer had an Hispanic last name, or was visually African-American, or was a varsity athlete. Virtually all of them were set-asides, students who had been let in either directly, or with a one-year time lag through NAPS. I cast my research net wider. The rest of the slowest students in the class, those keeping their noses above the magic line of C and about whom as a result I did not have to write reports, were also overwhelmingly set-asides.

Slow learners the Academy had gone out of its way to put in my classroom were making it impossible for me to make much headway with anybody. Teaching English to plebes is only secondarily teaching facts about literary history, which is of admittedly minor use in the fleet. We use literature to teach leadership, as well as thinking and expression skills. And those skills I know to be of major, not minor, use in the fleet, and anywhere else.

Individually, many of these weak students melt your heart. When they're sitting in front of you pouring out their hopes and dreams, you root for them, no matter how badly they perform. You want them to succeed. But empathy only goes so far. What about the high-scoring, highly motivated applicants who aren't sitting there? I'd much sooner have those applicants, who didn't get in, making decisions for sailors and Marines, rather than the ones we let in in their stead.

By letting in so many slow students for political or athletic reasons and pushing them along from semester to semester—students who are almost guaranteed to be at or below our minimum level of teachability—we are saying that the lives of the men and women they will be responsible for matter less to us than, say, our being able to field a winning basketball team. To be sure, lives depend on many other things too, like what the enemy does, and dumb luck. But the assumption behind educating officers-to-be is that their skills do matter. If they don't, we should all give up right now.

A somewhat grim devil's advocate might argue that all this is as it should be: we don't really want the smart ones. They'll be most uncomfortable with the strictures of our institution. It may be true that livelier students will be aware of its paradoxes. But in my book, that's a good thing.

The storm the Dean threatened (or was it merely prophesied?) as a result of my effrontery never broke over me. A week or so later, the Annapolis *Capital* was full of an investigation being carried out by the Navy's inspector general regarding a New Year's Eve incident at the Naval Academy Gate involving none other than our short-fused Superintendent. The story quickly reached the *Baltimore Sun* and the *Washington Post.*

Given that all adults who enter the Naval Academy are required to show a picture ID in our post-9/11 security-conscious climate, signs to that effect are clearly posted. The Superintendent—via the grapevine, I hear he was drunk—apparently became bellicose when asked by the Marine guard for his ID as he entered on foot in the wee hours of the New Year, dressed in civilian clothes. Ultimately he taunted the guard and waved the ID in his face. The Marine reacted by reaching for his pepper spray. The guard was later transferred out of the Naval Academy to Washington. Clearly our Admiral believed that RHIP: Rank Has Its Privileges. Rules are for the little people.

And then, miraculously, justice was done. The investigative body did its work and found that the Superintendent had struck the Marine Guard. The Admiral resigned the next day. The Navy always explains problems by speaking of "bad apples." But problems are almost always more systemic.

The Best and the Brightest

THE REASON WE take in so many weak students in preference to the better ones is, I reflect more and more often, our ideological commitment to the power of the individual to overcome all odds. In the conservative, and hence military, mindset, everything is a "choice," and motivation alone decides whether you succeed or fail. The only reason the Academy can accept to explain why a student is failing is that he or she isn't trying hard enough. Any other factors are irrelevant, and in any case are ruled out of court. The Academy just doesn't want to hear about them.

In the reports on students getting Ds and Fs, we're supposed to say why, in our view, they're doing unsatisfactory work. There's only one response the system wants to hear: the student isn't showing the proper motivation, not putting out the requisite effort. We're out of line if we suggest that motivation alone may not be the answer.

The semester with all the failing students, I found this out the hard way. Writing a report on one young man, a football player who couldn't think his way out of a paper bag and whose sentences were of the "See Spot run" variety, I pointed out that he had been admitted with SAT verbal scores a hundred points below what our minimum was supposed to be. That, I suggested, was the pretty obvious reason why he was so inept in my class.

The deans howled, I heard through my department chairwoman. The young man's company officer objected in person. I was being "unprofessional" in expressing the opinion that this particular midshipman was working with a disadvantage that no "motivation" would overcome—or at least, apparently had not overcome. But if they think that anyone can be motivated to succeed, why look at things like grades and scores at all in admissions? Why crow about the number of people who are rejected? "Ten to one!" a former superintendent liked to boast, referring to the ratio of applicants to seats. "Better than Harvard!"

The Academy's attitude that personal motivation alone determines all outcomes is so dogged that it sometimes becomes frightening, rather than merely frustrating. Several years ago I had as a student a young man, a senior English major, whose failing first paper in my course brought him to my office for a session of what we call E.I., "Extra Instruction." Annapolis is one of the few institutions in the world where students have access to professors just because they ask for it: if they want an hour of our time, they get it. Here, tax dollars really are at work.

Typically the student comes in with an unsatisfactory paper

(some come because they can't think of anything to write: we talk). Usually I turn the failing paper facedown, and simply ask the student what main point or points he or she was trying to get across. It almost invariably makes sense. Then we look at the failing paper, where—surprise!—it turns out that these ideas aren't so clearly laid out, though the student invariably thought they had been. The student typically sees this, and leaves able to fix the problem.

But this E.I. session did not go as they usually do. This young man looked at me intently, asked a question that betrayed he'd understood nothing of what I had just said (itself a repetition of what he'd already heard in the classroom) and waited expectantly for me to re-teach once more the material on which the paper was to be based. For a minute or two, trying to act in the "never give up" spirit of the institution, I rose to the bait, though my voice sharpened as I talked. Then, slowing, I asked him to carry on in his own words, to summarize something he'd now heard for the third time. He was silent, then tried to begin, then fell silent again.

"Excuse me a minute," I said. I turned away from him and pulled up his record on the computer: it was a mass of failed and repeated courses. His SAT scores were, for a white boy, rock-bottom. (Later he told me he'd taken them a dozen times; what's recorded and used in admissions is a mix-and-match pairing of the highest score on each part, whenever this was achieved.) When I asked a moment later, he told me he'd become an English major because he'd been getting Cs in his English courses rather than the Ds and Fs he was receiving in other courses.

"Look," I finally said, turning back to him. "An E.I. session isn't supposed to be about me teaching the material again just for you. What *did* you understand of what I said in class?"

And then it all comes out: nothing. He is in despair, apparently eager to confess his cluelessness. "Sir, I don't understand anything."

"Nothing?" I ask, unbelievingly.

"No, sir," he says.

What am I supposed to say to this?

"It's not like I don't try," he hurries on. "I spent hours on this paper. I just don't understand what you say in class." And then the floodgates open: his sense of having to fake it in class after class, his inability to get even the faintest glimmer of the main idea of the text, the torture of sitting in class while it all washes over him, his endless sessions of E.I. with professors accustomed to giving E.I. until they are blue in the face, class after class, semester after semester, that had allowed him to get this far.

"I've always had problems understanding the point of what I read," the young man, now brutally open with me, offers.

"I don't know what other people are thinking," he adds miserably.

And suddenly I had him pegged.

"I think you have Asperger's Syndrome—mild autism," I tell him bluntly. I explain to him what it is. I make educated guesses about his life, his symptoms. He looks at me as if I am a magician, nodding, interrupting me to agree. He is touchingly cooperative, apparently for the first time talking to someone with whom he doesn't have to pretend.

I see no reason to pull the punch. He is at the end of his rope, and I of mine—not to mention the system at the end of its. I tell him pleasantly that in my educated but nonprofessional opinion, he has a learning and cognitive disability that should be professionally evaluated. There are strategies for dealing with Asperger's, if no outright cure. One of the hallmarks of even mild autism is lack of empathy for others. "Aspies," as they are sometimes called, just don't understand how other people think—a very real danger in a command situation.

I add that I don't think he should be an officer in the Navy, and I'll have to say so in my six-week report. We're asked explicitly to give a recommendation: retain or separate. Only we can't say: "separate because of intrinsic unsuitability," only "separate because he has a bad attitude."

This is the institution that continually talks about how not making a rack (bed) properly leads to loss of lives. How much worse is it to let loose in the fleet someone with impaired cognitive faculties? Perhaps we could say, assuming I chose not to pursue it and merely let him scrape through the Academy the way he'd scraped through this far, that the likelihood was high that his superiors would at some point realize he was different. They might not know why, but they'd know. And they'd assign him to a desk job. But what guarantee do we have of that? If the Academy passed the buck, why wouldn't people in the fleet?

In any case, I told my student, he is abusing the E.I. system, which wasn't set up to take care of people who needed such massive intervention. It is meant as an occasional aid for students who basically get the point. He needs much more structured and concentrated intervention. But I can't guarantee that the Academy can accommodate his needs. I don't know that we have the facilities. Graduation is not guaranteed.

At this he becomes upset: his parents will never accept this. They will sue the Academy if the Academy tries to throw him out. They have worked their fingers to the bone. Even when others suggested that he had problems, his parents have always insisted there is nothing wrong with him.

At the mention of other people who suggested that he had problems, my ears perk up. Of course, I think, both ruefully and with relief, I'm not the first person to notice. I don't have to carry this whole burden by myself.

"Were these suggestions followed up?" I ask. "Have you ever been tested?"

He comes clean on this too. It turns out I'm not even the first person to flag him as a likely case of autism-spectrum disorder. A history professor who oversaw his work last year wrote countless e-mails to the powers-that-be demanding that he be tested. They were ignored.

I unload on our department chairwoman, who calls admissions. They assure her stiffly that we do not admit people with learning disabilities. Therefore, this young man cannot have such disabilities.

I begin writing e-mails to deans, explaining both how unfair it is to this young man and how potentially dangerous it is to the Navy to ignore what seems such a likely diagnosis.

The response comes back: testing would be a black spot on his record. They won't do it.

I respond by saying there would be no more Band-Aid E.I. sessions, since they are creating a false picture of normalcy. I explain that I'm not doing the student, or the Navy, a favor by teaching and re-teaching the material to him one-on-one, so that he can squeak through once again by memorizing enough to pass a test. This, I later learn, is deemed "unprofessional," the adjective used when the military doesn't know what to make of something.

I contact my colleague in the history department, who is sympathetic and corroborates my reactions and the E.I. experience, but tells me she has no illusions: she's gotten exactly the same reaction. I'm just the next in line to be told that all our students are fine, and that motivation is all.

The young man himself lets it be widely known that I don't "like" him. At that I have to acknowledge myself bested. It is the ultimate trump in a system that insists the individual can achieve anything he wants. My objections to him could, in such a system, be merely individual as well. I accept his painfully cobbled-together Potemkin-village memorizations as adequate for a passing grade. He duly graduates from the Naval Academy, and so far as I know, is in the Navy today. It'll take most people a while to figure out what they're looking at, and by then he may have served his time—if everyone is lucky, without being responsible for any deaths. At what point will we let go of our dogma that individual effort determines all and face the fact that it doesn't?

Another young man of a few years ago provided an even more chilling example of the downside to the system's dogged assertion that motivation alone determines performance. He was very bright, but clearly strange. He'd go without sleep for days on end, he told me, talk a mile a minute in my presence, free-associate, and carry on verbally as if flying high on something illegal—or as if afflicted by what used to be called manic-depression, now called bipolar disorder. He took to writing ten-page e-mails to professors, nothing suggestive or inappropriate, just wild flights about James Joyce.

This time a lot of people, at least in the English department, thought this young man was acting strange. I wrote e-mails to the deans suggesting what, in layman's terms, might be afoot. For everyone's safety, including his own, surely he should—I suggested—be professionally tested. Once again, no one would hear of this. Merely visiting a psychologist was bad for his career, being tested was the end of the road. All midshipmen were fine. Perhaps he should get more sleep.

This young man graduated too, only in this case I know what happened next. The specialty school—Nuclear Power—noticed that he wasn't sleeping and that he talked too fast. No buck-passing there; too much was at stake. By now an ensign, my ex-student was tested and determined to be, in fact, bipolar. The Navy discharged him.

Annapolis had insisted that he was "good to go."

Classical and Romantic

A FAVORITE TEXT of midshipmen at the Naval Academy is Theodore Roosevelt's speech on the subject of "Citizenship in a Republic" given in 1910 in Paris, whose central image is that of the "Man in the Arena." Indeed, the relevant excerpt was printed until recently as part of *Reef Points*, the book of facts and Naval Academy lore that plebes must memorize. It's the credo of the man of action.

> It is not the critic who counts, not the man who points out how the strong man stumbled, or where the doer of deeds could have done better. The credit belongs to the man who is actually in the arena; whose face is marred by the dust and sweat and blood; who strives valiantly; who errs and comes short again and again; who knows the great enthusiasms, the great devotions and spends himself in a worthy cause; who at the best, knows in the end the triumph of high achievement, and who,

at worst, if he fails, at least fails while daring greatly; so that his place shall never be with those cold and timid souls who know neither victory or defeat.

Harsh, as my students would say. But completely untrue? It implies something the Naval Academy has made conceivable to me, that there are two types of people: actors and thinkers. Sometimes I think of these as congruent to conservatives and liberals, respectively. At other times, I understand the Naval Academy better as a result of considering a distinction between Classical and Romantic made by the early-twentieth-century English poet T.E. Hulme, in an essay called "Classical and Romantic." According to Hulme, the two points of view can be contrasted through their relation to a common image, that of a well and the bucket that descends within it.

Romantics, Hulme suggested, see people as being like the well. They are fonts of infinite possibility. To realize these possibilities, one has only to dip in the bucket. For the Classicists, by contrast, a person is more akin to the bucket than to the well. Like the bucket in contrast to the well, they are extremely limited, and "it is only by tradition and organization that anything decent can be got out" of them.

In the Romantic view, little direct intervention is needed to develop a human being's possibilities. In the Classical view, a relaxation of vigilance over people leads to a reduction in productivity, and complete negligence would result in a breakdown: humans would cease to do anything at all. For the Romantic, we may say, the default speed of humans is a naturally fast speed. People will go forward all by themselves if we remove obstacles from their path. Think of the St. John's mission statement. For the Classicist, humans' natural speed is zero. They must constantly be both goaded on and prevented from erring from the preordained path. They must be aimed at something: think of the Academy's mission statement.

The Naval Academy, in Hulme's sense of the terms, is, therefore, a Classical institution. Yet it is a Classical institution set in and dependent on a Romantic society, its paradoxes and confusions due to the contrast between the two halves of the symbiosis. The membrane dividing the two is porous. Those people inside the Classical enclosure were, only shortly before, outside in the Romantic world. Most return to the outside for greater or lesser periods of time. Ultimately, they may rejoin the outside. And insiders, whether temporary or permanent, are at all times dependent on the outsiders for their livelihood. Yet though the traffic back and forth between viewpoints is by definition fluid, the viewpoints themselves remain, at some level, antithetical.

Many people find what goes on at the Naval Academy—or indeed, in any military environment—very strange indeed. How could anyone want to be bullied, humiliated, told what to do, put in a situation that is clearly the very antithesis of freedom? How could anyone voluntarily choose this situation, save those whose desires nature had so stunted as to wither them before their time? This objection is an expression of the Romantic viewpoint. It looks at the undeniable fact that our students are much more circumscribed in their actions, their dress, their behavior, and their choices than other young people their age; this is held to be an unmitigated evil. From this follows the simple disbelief that anyone could do this to anyone else, or that anyone would willingly submit to it. It must be sadism on the part of those who perpetrate the system, and masochism on the part of those who accept it.

The Classical viewpoint sees things quite differently: far from the uniforms, the drills, the "Yes, sirs" and "No, sirs" circumscribing freedom, they are instead a skeleton holding up flesh and preventing us from ending up in a pile on the floor, like jellyfish. At the very least, they are a series of hurdles that incite people to greater and greater achievement. The assumption is that without such admittedly onerous goads, very little would be accomplished. Of course you should wake people up at 0530. If you let people sleep till noon, they will, and then the day is half gone.

The Romantic sees a series of impediments to freedom in the endless list of tasks to be accomplished in a day at the Naval Academy. The Classicist responds that these present constant challenges and offer students a chance to excel. Yes, objects the Romantic, a chance to excel at goals that the individuals themselves had no hand in setting, constructed so as to be all but impossible to meet. Our students, to the Romantic, seem like rats being trained in mazes, mice being given walls that, experiments have shown, they can just barely manage to pull themselves over, squeaking all the way.

For the Classicist, we achieve true freedom through abnegation, through blending into the whole, achieving goals that a long line of people before us have achieved, that a group is achieving with us, and that those who follow us will have to achieve as well. Only submit, says the Academy: there are no leaders who have not first learned how to follow. At any rate, a life full of goals postulated and met is better than a life such as the vast majority of people lead, with no goals at all.

The transcendence of self demanded by military institutions is like the leap of faith required of someone entering a religious community. The monk or nun becomes free by giving up the material things of the world, and discovers his or her true nature by offering the self upon the altar of God, or Jesus, or the Mother Superior. The postulant forsakes commitments to other individuals, and takes vows of poverty, chastity, and obedience. To the outsider, it looks as if all is lost in this great giving-up of personal responsibility. To the insider, all is gained.

A Sense of Honor

THE MIDS ARE FOND of a novel, or perhaps rather a thinly disguised polemic, about Academy values written by alumnus and former Secretary of the Navy James Webb, called *A Sense of Honor*. The story turns on a realization scene wherein a recalcitrant plebe suddenly understands the spirit of the institution and becomes one of its most impassioned defenders rather than fighting its influence upon him. The villain in this book is a civilian professor. He lords his job over his acquaintances, saying that, as a professor at the Academy—this is during the Vietnam War—he cannot be drafted.

Webb's plebe-hero has been indoctrinated, today we would say harassed, by an upperclassman who has taken him on as a "project." The upperclassman already Understands. The pivotal scene, the plebe's epiphany, occurs when, as punishment for some infraction, the plebe is ordered to sleep naked on the metal webbing that holds up his mattress. The upperclassman gone, our plebe considers placing a sheet between his tender genitals and the metal that threatens to castrate him. (Obviously, he sleeps on his stomach.) He inserts the sheet and then, in a heroic gesture, removes it, though there is little likelihood that anyone will ever know whether he did so or not. He has made the leap of faith: he is following orders merely because they are orders. The right thing for its own sake: suffering for God alone. Rightness because of principle, not because of another human being: in fixing our sights beyond the transitory, we both give everything up and gain it back. For the Christian, what is gained back is life eternal; for the True Believers at the Naval Academy, it is military glory, or a knowledge that one has the Right Stuff (to use Tom Wolfe's phrase), or simply a kind of purity of action.

For Classicists, the military life is an end in itself; defense of a Romantic society is merely its side effect. This much should, I think, be admitted at least behind closed doors, if not to the world at large. The result of being clear about this would be a lessening of the wounded pride that characterizes the military. To the Romantic, customs whose sole purpose is to define the Classical (military) sub-unit will seem very silly indeed. But not to the Classical sub-unit itself. The Romantic question is: What do such repeated group activities as traditions or customs bring to the individual? The answer for the Romantic being "nothing," the customs are rejected. But the fact is that both Classicists and Romantics could agree, if they only cared to, that the answer to this question is "nothing." The Classicist, however, would go on to find rather banal the fact that of course such actions do nothing for the individual. That's not the point. They are meant to subsume the individual in the collective, in which s/he finds his or her true place. The purpose of customs and traditions isn't the actions themselves, as Romantics imagine. It's the shared act of doing them again, and together.

Of course it can be very painful; self-abnegation always is. I have come on countless plebes weeping into telephones in the basement of the library. For the Romantic, individual pain and suffering are absolute ills. For the Classicist, the only relevant question is, What do they accomplish? Usually the response is: we prove that we can survive them. For the Romantic, this is not enough. I think of Nelson Mandela's description of his circumcision as a young teenager: he writes that it took him several agonized moments to clear his head of the pain and to remember that he was supposed to yell a cry that means, "So now I am truly a man!" At the time, he remembers, he was ashamed that other boys put aside their pain many seconds before he did and shouted out the ritual phrase. This too is a ceremony where bearing pain marks the entrance into manhood, in a system set up by adults removed enough from their own pain that they have forgotten it, or if not, see no reason why others should forgo what they themselves underwent. It would be easy anthropology to cast the Naval Academy in terms of the manhood rituals of less technologically advanced peoples: virtually all societies are alike in prizing strength and endurance in males.

The outsider can't understand the military, because the military doesn't want to be understood by the civilian world. If it were, it would have to alter so that incomprehension once again reigned. Otherwise, how to preserve its identity in an alien world? Else why would the Marines be "the few, the proud"? In the military, you earn the right to be unlike the world outside, a world you ostensibly exist to defend. Thus the biggest paradox of all: those who willingly join a Classical structure in a Romantic world are themselves the greatest of the Romantics.

Everyone should be clear that the military way of life exists for its own sake, as a Classical substructure, an alternative to the world outside. This is why the military never worries too much about the things that drive, say, protesters into the streets, whether being used for a good or bad end. Why should they? They can't do anything about it. Far better to focus on things they can control—like individual valor—and defend their own, say against protesters. When the plebes say good night to Jane Fonda, as they do every night during plebe summer ("Good night, Jane. Good night, bitch!"), they are expressing their realization that the military exists for its own sake. Those who question them are worse than those they fight: they need the ones they fight to justify their existence.

The self-proclaimed pacifist William James began a 1910 essay entitled "The Moral Equivalent of War" by acknowledging that the military virtues of discipline, self-denial, and self-sufficiency held great worth. He was troubled, however, by the fact that these qualities seemed to thrive and be produced only within the context of structures whose purpose was to kill. He suggested it might be possible to encourage these virtues in another context, and proposed an idea that has taken on some contemporary resonance: a kind of national Service Corps, where "gilded youth" could do service to their country rather than remaining idle, and develop some of these undeniable virtues without the over-structure that had rendered them, in James's eyes, so noxious.

To Classicists, it is counterintuitive to think that people will be this self-denying for any goal less than an extreme one, a goal involving ultimate sacrifices and the highest stakes. You get people to perform at truly top form only as a result of threatening them with real threats and giving them real goals. Classicists understand that this involves the sacrifice of personal desires, personal wants, and perceived needs—indeed, of the individual. It's just that this doesn't seem too great a loss, these things being ephemeral to begin with. I too doubt that a system can generate this degree of self-denial with softer threats—which is not to say that individuals cannot achieve these virtues outside of a system.

If Classical and Romantic are, at least theoretically, polar opposites, the number of people who are convinced proponents of any worldview at all, whether Classical or Romantic, are in the tiny minority. Some plebes, like the hero of Webb's strangely moving fable—moving for reasons largely unintended by the author, I think—accept the collective in this way and find freedom, achieving the equivalent of a military Vocation. They are, my experience suggests to me, in the minority both at Annapolis and in the military in general.

Others refuse it. They too are in the minority, though I know some of them. One student of a few years ago was much affected by our reading of Wilfred Owen's "Disabled," about a triple amputee and war casualty. When I heard from him again, he had withdrawn from the Academy and was applying to civilian schools.

Most of our students are somewhere in the middle. They try to understand what those with a Vocation are explaining to them, but cannot. Neither do they, by and large, have the ability to refuse this vast machine that tells them quitting is a sign of moral decay. So they go with the flow, checking off the boxes, trying to do well, somehow dealing with not doing well, staying alive.

What should the Naval Academy be? Our answer to this question will be determined by whether we are fundamentally Romantic or Classical. For those of a Classical bent, even questioning the system is evidence of Romanticism. What is, is good. Classicists would like to be able to deny that all structures, even Classical ones, are constructed by individuals.

Yet the strange fact of life is that Classicism implies Romanticism, as Romanticism is the rebellion against Classicism. Perhaps the two are most properly seen, as Hulme himself implied, not as historical designations or even conflicting worldviews, but as the yin and yang of all our psyches, the two poles that define humanity. And that means that we must get used to disagreements and oscillations between them.

Even the Classicist must not come to believe too implicitly his or her own claims, and the Romantic must understand where his or her emphasis on the individual may lead. This means that we need to continue to talk with each other.

Quibbles over the precise degree of tension in the Academy program such as we are currently engaged in (should second-classmen be allowed to touch plebes? Should we make first-classmen go to breakfast?) take up a great deal of time, and probably provide the bulk of the arguments between the Classicists and the Romantics. They are trivial arguments in purely intellectual terms, a question of fine-tuning.

We all, whether Classical or Romantic, conservative or liberal, would therefore, I think, do well to heed a text that was for many years included in *Reef Points,* and that was memorized by plebes. It is part of a speech "delivered 1 August 1975 by William P. Mack, Vice Admiral, USN, USNA Class of 1937, upon completion of his duty as 47th Superintendent of the U.S. Naval Academy," as the Class of 1998 edition puts it (pages 34–35). That was the last year this speech was included in *Reef Points.*

> As I complete 42 years of service, I would like to leave to the Brigade of Midshipmen a legacy of one idea which represents the distillation of that experience: . . . The one concept which dominates my mind is that of the necessity of listening to and protecting the existence of the "Dissenter"—the person who does not necessarily agree with his commander, or with popularly-held opinion, or with you. Unfortunately, history is full of examples . . . [of people who] eventually succeeded, but not with the help of patient, understanding naval officers. Regretfully, each needed help from outside the uniformed navy. . . .
>
> The point is: To begin at an early age to cultivate an open mind to determine to hear all arguments and opinions, no matter how extreme they may seem, and, above all, to preserve and protect those who voice them.

Alma Mater

IN 1997, WHEN I published a novel, I was invited back to my alma mater, Haverford, to speak. The campus looked as serene as it always had, the ducks swimming on the duck pond as they had done before, or as their great-great-duckfathers and -mothers before them had. My entryway, as we called the divisions of the L-shaped Lloyd Hall, where I lived in my senior year, was unchanged, though there were signs that other people lived there now: the living room didn't look a bit the way it should have.

A handful of new buildings had gone up since my time, including the student center with a few guest rooms, where they put up us speakers. But the library seemed unchanged: the same Maxfield Parrish (Haverford 1892) painting in the same place as before, the same fountain splashing on the tiles. Even the man behind the desk was literally the same man as a quarter-century before, save for the fact that his black hair had been struck snow-white.

I did the obligatory nostalgic wander through classrooms where I had sat late at night, alone with the fluorescent lights on, poring over my Wittgenstein; the dorm where I'd lived in my junior year; the dining hall, with the same huge and horrible 1960s painting in the atrium fireplace. The amazing thing about my jog that evening around the campus was how short it was, how quickly I circumnavigated the whole. Yet of course the spaces of our youth always look smaller and pokier when we become adults.

For me, college was an endless voyage into the caves of the self. Probably it could have happened anywhere. Perhaps it was almost by chance that that voyage happened here among the ginkgo trees that dropped their fruit in the fall—like those by the side of the Naval Academy's parade field whose scent turns me nostalgic—and turned the flagstones rotten with a reminder of mortality, flagstones that led us on to interiors warm with lights, sherry, intense discussions of Plato and the Meaning of It All. How can I forget, though now it is decades after the fact, my favorite philosophy professor leaning over the table in our Aristotle seminar, grinning to himself at the hoary conclusion he was about to present to us, dropping his voice to a whisper and opening his eyes to emphasize his point: "Virtue is its own reward," he whispered. "Virtue is its own reward."

The next morning, after my speaking engagement, I was invited to teach a creative-writing class. The students were bright, as I'd expected. What I wasn't prepared for was my reaction to the way they looked and sounded, so much weaker in self-presentation than my own other-directed students back at Annapolis. The boys wore baseball caps, mostly backwards. The girls (this was a mixture of male and female Haverford students and the by-definition female Bryn Mawr undergraduates) sported multiple piercings in their ears and elsewhere, as did some of the boys. There was no evidence of recent haircuts. They slumped in their chairs.

I was horrified, as much by my own reaction as by what I saw. What a sucker I had clearly become for my hulking, fresh-faced mids, snappily dressed, smiling, outgoing, and ready to lead! The quotient of "like"s in these elite college students' speech was alarmingly high as well. As in, "I'm, like, unaware of any, like, discrepancy here." After class I confessed my reaction to the colleague who'd invited me. "Doesn't it drive you crazy?" I asked. "At Annapolis, I won't let them do that. I hold up fingers for the number of times they say 'like' and write a 'like-busters' sign on the board and point to it as they talk. I tell them that talking like that diminishes their authority, and that they have to get rid of it to be effective as officers. Which," I finished somewhat defensively, "happens to be true."

"Yes," she agreed. "It does drive me crazy. But it wouldn't be kosher to say anything to them. It would be considered an infringement on their personal rights." I couldn't tell if she said this proudly or ruefully. At any rate, it was clear the subject was closed.

However they looked or sounded, I had to believe that these students were younger versions of me; that the place had not changed so much in a mere quarter-century. In fact, probably they were me precisely because of the way they looked, if not for the "like"s, which in my time were not yet in vogue. At their age, I reminded myself, I didn't work out and didn't own a suit. I went to class in ratty tennis shoes, just like they did. And my graduation picture shows me wearing an embarrassing beard and needing a haircut.

So what? What did it matter what I looked like? Or if I was outgoing? There was time for all that later. Haverford was the place where I found out who I really was. That was what I understood to be my job in college, and by the time I graduated I had done it. Not a hundred percent, of course: life still had some surprises in store for me. But, I'd say, eighty-five percent. And once you find yourself eighty-five percent, you can turn at least some of your attention to other things. Or, rather, other people.

I think people are meant to pass through inner-direction so that they can achieve outer-direction. If you start too early with outward-direction, it leaves you rudderless all your life, unable to relate in a stable way to anyone else.

Most of my students encounter reality for the first time when they leave Annapolis. Suddenly they must prepare their own food, do their own laundry, make their own time-management decisions, and possibly even negotiate the uncharted waters of living with someone of the opposite sex. Most of the marriages contracted in the weeks after graduation in the chapel end in divorce, and not merely because of the rigors of military life and its incompatibility with domestic life. Young officers—eternal adolescents—act out their rebellion at places like the Tailhook convention. Some of them stay in the military till they are close to thirty. Increasingly nowadays they are released against their will, and have to redefine themselves in a world they have not been part of for many years. Those who stay in for a full twenty-year career get out in their early forties; at this point, the transition to doing things themselves seems even more difficult.

Most midshipmen, for all their complaining, love their restraints. One source of stress is the criminalization of sex in the Hall: sex between upperclass and plebes, and sex between members of their own company, even elsewhere. At Annapolis, this is called "fraternization," "frat" for short—the same as sexual relations in the active-duty military. I think: sex can probably be controlled for short periods of time under intense or exceptional conditions. It's the fond dream of the military that these exceptional conditions can be generalized into a rule holding good for four years—or in some cases, for life.

For heaven's sake! I sometimes say to them. You're twenty years old, full of hormones, and you live on top of each other. Of course you want to have sex in the Hall! If you don't bother your roommates and show up for class, who cares whether or not you do?

"But, sir!" they protest. And they're off, explaining to me that Bancroft Hall is like a ship (except that no tour of duty is four years long), and of course you can't have sex on a ship (though many people do: some women always come back pregnant, not to mention what might—the horror!—be going on between the men). What they love, like monks their pallets of straw, is precisely the comforting sense of the privations closing them in, keeping them secure.

"You can't have the administration approving of sex in the Hall!" they say. "Everything would fall apart!"

"Having no position on the matter isn't the same as approving of it," I respond. For them, of course, it is, as for any good Classical or conservative thinker. Failing to police something means tacitly condoning it. It's the same argument they give me against gay marriage: they can, at the limit, accept that gay people are having sex; they just don't want official acknowledgment that it's happening—and for them, marriage equals sex, so allowing marriage means condoning sex. What you don't admit exists doesn't exist. You can't just leave something alone.

I point out that for many decades civilian colleges have had no opinion about sex in dormitories, and that somehow education has not been affected. Besides, I say, you don't have to have sex if you don't want to. But putting the decision back on the individual is the death knell of all Classical, and conservative, substructures, such as the military or the Academy. If it's up to me, then where are the rules? If that's how we do things, this might as well be Chesapeake University, as I heard one Marine grousing to another in the weight room. The midshipmen grouse too. But they'd fight anyone who tried to "liberate" them. One of my students, a prior, quoted to me a saying from his time in the fleet: "a bitchin' sailor is a happy sailor."

Yet people change over time. I heard recently about one of my students from the first year I was at Annapolis who was a very big man on campus indeed: strikingly handsome, pursued by all the women. He left in a blaze of glory; I remember his family of large Polynesian female relatives draping his immaculate choker whites with leis on graduation day. He tried to be a pilot, I hear, one of the sexiest things to do on leaving the Academy; report has it that he took to drink and washed out. Now I hear he has decided that he is gay. He's out of the Navy, having served his time, and is living the fast life in the Pacific.

Another, a stellar plebe from my early years at Annapolis, was a young man whose quickness and intelligence I admired. I wasn't at all surprised when, as a "firstie," a senior, he was named Brigade Commander. I lost track of him for a while, then heard that he had become a conscientious objector and had successfully fought the Navy to get out, rather than simply doing his five years without protest.

One day, there came a knock on my office door. I was correcting papers and got up to answer it. The door swung open to reveal a slightly older-looking but basically unchanged young man. I gave him a hug, he gave me one. We slapped each other on the back. We got reacquainted, caught up: his studies, my books and new family. After a time the conversation slowed, and I decided to chance it.

"Okay," I said. "Satisfy my curiosity. How do you go from being Brigade Commander to fighting the Navy as a conscientious objector?"

He sat back, smiled ruefully, was silent, tried to speak, then spread his hands in acknowledgment of the apparent paradox.

Finally he said, "There's no downtime. How are you ever going to reflect on things? It's like the Moonies. You know."

I did know. I remembered the blank-faced flower sellers that the Korean charlatan Sun Myung Moon used to send into American shopping malls in the 1970s and '80s, droopy, wild-eyed young men and women with pasted-on smiles. It was pos-

sible because of the miracle of sleep deprivation, as former ad-
herents later testified. Plus the desire of all these rootless young
people to be told what to do.

I think the Naval Academy offers most of our students what
most of them want: an exciting ride on a roller coaster that never
puts them down, that's enough of a challenge that they have to
hold on with both hands to keep from falling off, and that gives
them a sense of accomplishment when they once again set foot
on the ground four years later.

"They just don't want you to figure things out," the former
Brigade Commander told me. "Or at least," he added, trying to
be fair, "there just isn't time for you to do it."

Only later, when the roller-coaster ride is over, when the
bright lights are turned off and the people have gone home.
Only later, when the music stops.